A Collection of Canadiana

BEFORE SLICED BREAD

Jeannette Kerr

MEMOIRS & CUISINE

◆ FriesenPress

Suite 300 - 990 Fort St
Victoria, BC, Canada, V8V 3K2
www.friesenpress.com

Copyright © 2015 by Jeannette Kerr
First Edition — 2015

Painting on Front Cover by Carole Spandau.
www.carole-spandau.artistwebsites.com

ISBN
978-1-4602-6762-2 (Hardcover)
978-1-4602-6763-9 (Paperback)
978-1-4602-6764-6 (eBook)

1. Biography & Autobiography, Cultural Heritage

Distributed to the trade by The Ingram Book Company

CONTENTS

Foreword

Before Sliced Bread is a warm nostalgic walk down memory lane. A walk through the pre-
and post-war years in Canada, when life was simple and free. I can identify with Jeannette,
as I lived within the vicinity of which she writes. I taught Art in Montreal at Thomas Darcy
McGee High School and I took my teacher training at St. Joseph's Teacher's College on
Durocher Street, just a stone's throw from those duplexes with the iconic winding staircases
that I paint. It is exciting to stroll through the pages where I too grew up as a child. Jeannette
captures the very essence of that era and what it means to be Canadian. Many of the family
businesses are still there today, Schwartz's Deli on the Main, Wilensky's Diner on Fairmount,
Beauty's Luncheonette on Mont Royal and our yummy bagel shops on St. Viateur and
Fairmount. These delicious Montreal Memories come to life when you read the pages of
Jeannette's lively and exciting new book. *Before Sliced Bread* touches on the Acadia expulsion,
the Maritimes, Ontario and Western Canada. It flows like the maple syrup, which is one
of the symbols of our great nation along with the authentic family recipes, which in my
estimation makes this book a true slice of Canadiana! *Before Sliced Bread* is a treasure trove of
tasty tidbits. Take a bite out of this wonderful book, the recipes enthrall.

Carole Spandau
Montreal, Quebec
May 2015

DEDICATION

For my family and friends. For my dear daughters who waited patiently through the years for the release of this book, I dedicate to each and every one of you with love. For the characters in the stories, I rush towards completion before you all expire! For "Maggie and Jack", without them this book would not have been made possible. For John my loving husband who supported me through hours of proof reading, photographs and through one of his most delightful tasks, the taste testing of each recipe in this book! In memory of my sweet son Terry who used to say I was the greatest Mom in the whole world...no matter what! I miss you terribly. For my granddaughter Michelle, who helped me when I needed it most, and for all the "bestest" friends around world!

*"Say it loud, say it clear
you can listen as well as you hear
It's too late when we die
To admit we don't see eye to eye"*

"The Living Years"
—Mike and the Mechanics

Introduction

"We may live without poetry, music and art.
We may live without conscience, and live
Without heart;
We may live without friends; we may live
Without books;
But civilized man cannot live without cooks."

—*Owen Meredith*

"The greatest thing *since* sliced bread" was a popular expression brought on by Mr. Otto Rohwedder of Iowa, USA. He invented the first bread slicer in 1928. Ever since, this idiom has been associated with anything that betters life in general.

"*Before* sliced bread" however, is a metaphor. One which encompasses the long arduous history that forged the future, so that everyone to this present day may now have the privilege to utter those famous words, "The greatest thing since sliced bread." Hence, *Before Sliced Bread* is a collection of anecdotes, history, and authentic recipes.

Being a Canadian woman and fiercely proud of my heritage, I take pride in sharing my journey with you, back to a time when things were simple and life was reverent. It was an age of innocence. It reflects the stories of a young child growing up in Canada during WW II in the late 1930s until the present day. It encapsulates Canada, commencing with the Acadian Expulsion in 1755 and crosses the country from the province of Newfoundland and Labrador to the Yukon Territory.

Our forefathers, those courageous pioneers from other lands, who taught us how to till the land, drain the marshes, dry the fish, build the boats, grow the wheat, and make the bread, brought their traditions, culinary skills and marvelous recipes. These authentic recipes are included through the chapters. The threads that I drew for the stories and recipes in this book, I took from the fabric of my life, a life woven from the hemp of Irish, French, and Acadian culture and the peoples of this great land of ours called Canada!

For the benefit of the reader, I would like to illustrate that I wrote parts of this book through the eyes of a child... a child not concerned with the fundamental viewpoint of economics, religion, nor the complexities of the era, but as a child who lived through the hard times... but never knew it!

The Start

∽◦ MOVING TO THE BIG CITY ◦∽

It was the fall of 1938. The Canadian National Railway's "Ocean Limited" chugged its way into Montréal's Bonaventure station, after a long overnight trip that left the simple little town of Dalhousie, New Brunswick far behind.

I was only a child and oblivious to the fact that Hitler had just declared war on Poland and that my father was one of the fortunate few to acquire a good job during these depressed times.

I on the other hand, was more interested in the sounds of "Sweeesh-shoo… sweeesh-shoo… ka-chunk… ts-s-s-s-s-s" of the big choo-choo train. It slowly came to a screeching halt, spewing hot steam through the open window at my brothers and I, making us giggle with delight. We watched in wide-eyed wonder as the long wooden platform swarmed with people greeting each other, embracing, laughing, running and dragging suitcases behind them. As young as I was, I do remember ladies wearing long slim coats and fancy plumed hats that bounced with every short perky step. This, my mother later recounted, was a sharp contrast to that of the down-and-outers with turned up collars and frayed fedoras, scanning the *Montréal Gazette* desperately searching for work.

Times were harsh. However, we were fortunate that my father held a position with the Dominion Engineering Company. Mesmerized by the unfamiliar clamor of all this, we clung to our mother's coat in fear of being swallowed into the droning beehive that was once called Ville-Marie.

"*Où est Daddy?*" We asked impatiently as our mother stood on tippy toes feverishly scanning the crowds. Her name was Marguerite, only twenty-six-years old, and already the mother of four little ones, a good start for a typical Catholic family from down east.

My mother's striking blue eyes quickened at her uncertain surroundings, but her strong French heritage compelled her to forget, for the time being, the quiet countryside and loving family she had left so far behind.

Above the crushing throng her face radiates delight as she spots the first and only man she has ever loved, her handsome beloved Jack. He stood tall, a brown fedora cocked saucily to the side of his head. The stubborn Irish Newfoundlander who couldn't or wouldn't learn to speak French.

"Margaret… my Maggie," he affectionately called out as he scooped her high into his young arms and kissed her passionately. She blushed with ecstasy. This universal language they both understood.

"*Ici les enfants*," my mother calls out as we pile into a cab for the long drive to our new flat on Hutchison Street. We watched as the cab slowly drove down our street with its stone triplexes and winding staircases, fronted by black wrought iron fences that guarded a small patch of grass.

"This – 5429 Hutchison Street – will be our new home in the Jewish quarter, where you will live, and learn how to speak English," my father said.

"*Et le français québécois aussi*," my mother answered smugly. She knows he does not understand a word she is saying and in turn, he nods his head approvingly.

As we pile out of our taxi we noticed some young boys dressed in black suits with one long ringlet poking out each side of their black-brimmed hats. This brought us into a stupefied stare. They spoke Yiddish, which was as foreign to us as the English language. We later learned that they were "Hassidic", a Jewish religious sect. They were to be amongst us as our new neighbours.

"A street where the boys have longer curls than I and don't even speak French," I wailed as I gripped my rag doll and silently cried into her blue wool hair. Even at that tender age I knew that I would never again run wild through the vast pristine field of forget-me-nots that grew right up next to my grandmother's house in New Brunswick.

Time is a child's best friend. It wasn't too long before Hutchison Street became a special street. Not because its maple trees were so tall and lush they formed a canopy of green that covered the street; not because it ran straight into Mount Royal. It was special because it's where our hearts lived; it was home, home for us as well as many others.

It encompassed a mosaic of ethnic groups. Names like Dumbrowski, Levitz, Handleman, and Schneider's appeared on storefronts everywhere. Streets were named for explorers like Clark and Durocher or the pioneering nursing sister Jeanne Mance.

On rue St-Viateur on the corner of St. Urbain Street stood St. Michael's Irish Catholic Church, where our family attended mass on Sundays and my brother Johnny was an altar boy. That was where we were baptized and made our first communion, confirmation, and where we prayed for our soldiers overseas and for the ones that never returned.

St. Michael's Church opened in 1915 and was predominantly Irish. It soon grew into the largest Anglophone parish in Montréal. It had a splendid high dome interior featuring a neo-renaissance style fresco of St. Michael watching the fall of the angels. Painted by Italian artist, Guido Nincheri, the fresco kept many a restless child in awe at its colourful splendour. In 1964, because of the large growth of the Polish community, the church expanded and inaugurated it as Church of St. Michael and St. Anthony, which it remains today.

One street that gained a little notoriety was St. Urbain Street where one of my favourite Canadian authors Mordecai Richler, was brought up as a boy. He used it as a focal point for his popular novel "St. Urbain's Horsemen." Among his best known works is "The Apprenticeship of Duddy Kravitz."

In his controversial book "Oh Canada! Oh Québec!" (a requiem for a divided country), He had publicly denounced the draconian language laws prohibiting English or bilingual signs in Québec, which did not garner him popularity, especially among the *"pur laine"*.

Mordecai recounts how he, as a boy, frequented the drugstore on the corner of Park Avenue and rue St-Viateur. In the book he couldn't recall its name. He tells of a kindly old French druggist who would invite him and his friends out back. There, he would patiently weigh out chemicals at the token price of thirty-five cents, just enough to create the ultimate stink bomb to throw at girls. I probably bumped into Mordecai in these early days and never knew it. I probably didn't want to either as we used the same druggist to create the same stink bombs that my girlfriend Mo and I used to throw at the fresh St. Urbain Street boys on our way to Luke Callaghan School on Clark Street!

In 1994, I met Mordecai Richler at a book signing at the University of British Columbia. He was promoting his new book "This Year in Jerusalem".

His imposing figure clad in a rumpled trench coat and chewing a fat stogie, made him appear rather "Colombo" like. I purposely queued to the back of the line, as I wanted a chance to converse with him. He signed a copy of his book for me, and we had a chuckle about the stink bombs. "You are right, now that I recall, it was Leduc's drugstore," which took him for a moment down a familiar path. He asked what "Before Sliced Bread" was (that I cunningly slipped under his nose). It was my manuscript; I requested him to sign it. He flipped through the pages and said, "Catchy title" and with that he signed his name across the front cover. Before parting he wished me "Good luck!" and said, "Never give up!"

Leduc's storefront faced Park Avenue. Here the *petit chars* (tramways) ran non-stop, some with a seductive portrait of a reclining Lili St. Cyr emblazoned on its side promoting her upcoming venue as an exotic burlesque dancer at the Gayety Theatre.

The *clang, clang!* tram bells punctuated the chants of the newspaper hawkers "La Presse… Montreal Star… read all about it…Churchill addresses the nation."

This Year in Jerusalem

Mordecai Richler

MORDECAI RICHLER

BEFORE

SLICED

..... BREAD

BY: JEANNETTE M. KERR

Mordecai Richler

Colourful newspaper stands dotted the street corners. They were covered in magazines and papers in neat little rows held together by wooden clothespins.

Inside the little stand an old lady adjusted her babushka. She huddled to keep warm in the cocooned layers of coats that sheltered her from the unyielding cold. Only her calloused fingertips poked out of frayed gloves enabling her to grasp the copper pennies she so desperately needed. She stopped only to blow warm air on her hands.

On the corner of Park Avenue and Bernard Street was the home of the famous Rialto Theatre with its hundreds of blinking lights. The marquee boasted stars like Shirley Temple, Claudette Colbert, Lionel Barrymore and Joseph Cotton.

I used to squint my eyes at those lights and pretend I was Shirley Temple dancing "On the good ship Lollipop" with long blonde ringlets – and not the skinny little girl I was with short, straight dark hair cut to resemble a German helmet.

Children were not allowed in the theatre in those days so on Saturdays it was off to the Talmud Torah school basement on Fairmont Street. We saw Hopalong Cassidy, Laurel and Hardy, "Bomba the Jungle Boy" and "Our Gang", on grainy black and white film, all for the kosher price of ten cents a head!

The back lanes of our street were special. I learned how to ride a two-wheeler, make a perfect twirly on roller skates, and walk on crushed tin cans, clunking all the way to the corner of rue St-Viateur.

But it was the sights and sounds that emanated from that narrow corridor that was so exciting for us children. The alley vendors plied their trade with the utmost tenacity.

First, came **The Ice Man**. You could hear the worn metal-rimmed wheels on the uneven pavement as the cart drew nearer, followed by the reverberating sound of the clip-clop of the scrawny horse's hooves. The wagon was long and slender with high sides. Large blocks of ice, covered with heavy canvas, stuck out the top. Bits of sawdust stuck to melting ice leaving a trail of cool water on hot pavement. A cool welcome sight to the many stray alley cats!

For twenty-five cents you watched the ice man pick up the block with large iron tongs after you chose a suitable piece. We always chose a bigger chunk so we could chip away at it catching flying splinters of ice shards and popping them into our mouths. He labored as he heavily stomped up the back stairs to the waiting icebox; this sound still evokes memories for my little brother Dougie as he nervously hid behind the door!

The Rag Man especially intrigued me. In the late afternoon we could hear a deep voice in the far distance calling, "Raaaags ah raaaags, old clothes, bottles, rags," he chanted. An old Jewish man with a battered black hat and a long white beard, he sat tall and proud, as if leading his people to the Promised Land. His wagon was junk-laden with old clothes, rags, bits of metal scraps, and just about anything you could buy, sell, or trade for a few pennies.

We never did much business with the rag man as my mother made and re-patched all our clothes, but he was part of the backyard parade that made life on Hutchison Street so interesting.

On Saturday mornings, we could hear the melodic singsong of Mario, **The Fruit and Vegetable Man**. "*J'ai des pommes, des carrottes, des navets,* and some cherries. *Des bananes,* cucumbers and berrrries, soma ripe soma not, you can have what I got… berrrries." (I have apples, carrots, turnips, cherries, bananas, cucumbers and berries.)

He wore a large straw hat garnished with carrot leaves, cherries, flowers, or whatever his mood allowed. He smiled a lot and I couldn't help but liken him to a male Carmen Miranda! The children followed him like the Pied Piper hoping he would throw them an apple or two. If he didn't, they'd help themselves to one when he wasn't looking!

Mom always sent us out to buy *des belle pommes* for *Poutine à trou*, an Acadian dessert. She would wrap pastry dough around some apples, insert brown sugar, cinnamon and raisins. When they came piping hot from the oven she poured a little brown sugar sauce over them. They were delicious, as delicious as the sights and sounds of my back yard!

POUTINE À TROU

In Québec French, *poutine* means pudding; *trou* means hole. This is a favourite dessert among French Acadians.

Make a double crust pastry recipe of your choice. Cut the dough into large circles (a dessert bowl makes a good template).

FILLING

3 cups peeled and diced apples	¼ cup brown sugar
½ cup raisins	2 tbsp melted butter
	2 tbsp cinnamon

Combine: Apples, raisins, sugar, and cinnamon. Fill each circle of pastry with this mixture. Bring the edges of the circle together and form a ball.

Turn the ball upside down on a greased cookie sheet, making sure the edges are well tucked underneath. Make a hole on top of each parcel, (I use a vanilla bottle cap) or poke a hole with your finger. Baste each one with beaten egg wash. Sprinkle with sugar. Bake at 400°F for about 30 minutes or until golden brown. Serve with:

BROWN SUGAR SAUCE

2 cups brown sugar	2 tsp cornstarch
2 tbsp butter	1½ tsp vanilla
¾ cups boiling water	

Melt butter in a medium-sized non-stick saucepan. Add sugar. Caramelize over high heat for one minute until dark brown. Add hot water and stir vigorously until sugar is melted. Stir in cornstarch, cook for another few minutes until thickened. (Add more cornstarch if you want a thicker consistency.)

Our new life in the city was simple yet complex. Discrimination was alive and well. There were the French versus the English; the Protestants versus the Catholics; and, everyone versus the Jews. There were Reform Jews and Orthodox Jews. Our kind Mr. Rosenberg was an Orthodox Jew who lived next door, wore a scull cap and touched the *mezuzah* affixed to the side of the door then reverently to his lips. A mezuzah has a paper scroll inside with a Hebrew prayer: "Hear O Israel, the lord our God is one... love the Lord your God and serve him with all your heart and soul."

The Protestants criticized the Catholics for practicing paganism – by adoring plaster statues – which they don't. The Catholic kids blamed the Anglicans for not believing in the Pope, and collectively we all blamed the Jews for crucifying Jesus Christ!

The Jewish kids watched in awe as we Catholics – the chosen People – (we took that quote from the Jews) flaunted "our" God encased in an ornate golden Monstrance (a vessel that contains a blessed host for veneration) in the annual opulent Corpus Christie Procession. Huge ribboned banners and multitudes of children paraded in their first communion regalia. Traffic was halted from Querbes to St. Urbain Street and Bernard to Fairmont. The parade passed the Jewish temple where the rabbis stood to watch the pomp of it all. I was chosen to hold the floating ribbon from a banner of the face of Christ. I thought, *If God placed all the unbaptized Catholic babies that died into "Limbo" then where will he put all the unbaptized Jews?* Oy vey!

We in turn scrutinized the Jewish faith and traditions such as the lavish preparations of Bar Mitzvah when a young man enters manhood. It was like a birthday and Christmas all rolled into one!

CORPUS CHRISTI PARADE

The Hassidic community remained impervious to the outside world and was repeatedly taunted for their ancient dress and ways. You could sometimes hear shouts of *maudit Juifs* (damn Jews) and *en bas les Juifs* (down with the Jews). Nonetheless they silently took it in stride as it was against their religion to rebuff. On Fridays, we watched them walk four abreast on Park Avenue speaking Yiddish, bobbing their heads up and down completely oblivious to their surroundings. They were a curious lot for us kids; however, it was very interesting.

Why did God create but one man? "So that no one of his descendants should say, 'my father is better than your father.'" Or, "My race is superior to yours."
—Sandhedrin, 37a.

As francophones, it didn't take us long to take command of the English language. We found out early what a "herring choker" meant (a Maritimer). We also learned a few Yiddish words to get by. My friend Moishe taught me some words to integrate into conversation.

Archie Bunker once said: "Jesus was a Jew , but only on his mother's side."

I recall an incident where a few neighbourhood boys were trying to impress Mr. Rosenberg with their Yiddish words. I breathlessly ran into him saying, "Hello, Mr. Rosenberg...*Gey in drere!*"

"Where did you learn to speak Yiddish so well, Jeannette?"

"Moishe, our Jewish friend taught me," I said proudly.

"*Vel,* Jeannette, in such a fantastic accent, you just told me to go to hell!"

Ish-kabibble! (So much for Yiddish.)

Racial prejudices in Montréal were everywhere. The long hot summer days made the children restless. Having the occasional *bataille royale* among rival neighbourhoods was not uncommon. The boys armed themselves with garbage can lids and marched down the lanes declaring war on the French, the English, Protestants, or Jews or whoever started name-calling. When boredom set in and the sight of a white rag waving on a stick, or "surrender" was scrawled on the back of a discarded "Vote for Duplessis" sign, we knew it was time for a truce.

Sometimes the bickering and stone throwing continued until it got dark. No one ever got badly injured in the scuffle. Despite cuts and bruises these same kids who threw rocks at each other still played hockey or ball the next day. These boys were the same ones that poked fun at our Acadian accents (after we called them shmucks), let it be known that our accent was not up to Québec's standards, but by the same token, Québec's accents were not up to France's standards either... or so we heard. My friend Monique was from Brittany, France and her mother felt that her language was by far more superior to that of Québec French. With childlike abandon, it reminded me of the big fish eating the little bitty fish and so on. I saw it all as a big pot of French pea soup with lots of Matzo balls floating on top!

❧ LILIES-OF-THE-VALLEY ❧

Although we had no daily interactions with our Jewish neighbour Mr. Rosenberg, he crept into our hearts ever so gently. He passed most of his time growing beautiful flowers in an otherwise small, unforgiving city garden. Perhaps it was to dim the reminders of a harsher time in his life, I don't know, but as a child I would hear whispers of, "She, (Mrs. Rosenberg) has the numbers on her arm," which was curious to me but not consuming. Auschwitz was not a term familiar to me.

Our backyard was devoid of any grass, save for the long spindly blades that hugged the unpainted fence. This was due partly to the roughhousing of my four brothers, but I had a secret. In the far corner and under the kitchen window, was a loose slat in the fence. There, every spring I would look for the early buds of the lilies-of-the-valley that spilled over from Mr. Rosenberg's flowerbed, and into our space. What joy! What heady perfume! I would push my skinny arms in deeper and amass enough flowers to fill a short Mason jar for the kitchen table. My mom would smile, as she knew it meant so much to me. I hid this flower oasis from my annoying brothers with a small board.

One Saturday morning, with Mason jar in hand, I neared the fence, only to see the board had been moved, the dirt roughened and not a lily-of-the-valley in sight. I was crushed, and oh so sad. *Little beggars,* I thought. I sat on the barren dirt and cried like a broken child. Reluctant to leave my small secret garden I slowly dragged myself into the house. A few days had passed when my mother asked if I had more flowers (I couldn't bear to tell her at the time). Through scalding tears I told her what happened. She went out to view the damage so the punishment could fit the crime, which suited me just fine.

"*Mon Dieu,* Jeannette, look 'eer!" my mother called out excitedly. With eyes wide, I rushed over to see an abundance of lilies-of-the-valley, nestled into a mound of fresh rich dark earth (a large shovel full no less). God must have heard my prayer!

Contemplating my thoughts, I suddenly heard quiet stirrings on the other side from where I stood. I was too little to see over the fence, so I knelt down and put my face to the ground and into the small opening and whispered, "Thank you, Mr. Rosenberg."

There was a long pause, then came a soft ... "Mazel tov, little one."

❧ RED RIVER COATS AND WINTER IN MONTRÉAL ❧

Every little girl in Québec wanted a Red River Coat. The design of the coat is derived from the clothing worn by the Métis in the 19th century. The Métis are a distinct Aboriginal people with a mixture of cultures of the First Nations, French Canadian,

English, and Orkney/Scottish. The Red River Coat was made of navy blue wool Melton with red-trimmed epaulettes and capuchin hood. With this we wore red woolen leggings, which we pulled over shoes and inside our boots. Completing the outfit was a bright red tasseled toque with matching red mittens on a string, and a woolen sash that wrapped around the waist at least twice. We all resembled little *Habitant* dolls. The school's cloak-room was a free-for-all, as we couldn't distinguish one pair of leggings or mittens from another. The coat kept a child warm, which was comforting, especially when you had to stand in line with ration tokens in hand for a pound of sugar.

Because this coat was wool, and not waterproof, it stood many a night drying on the back of a chair next to a rattling radiator.

Everyone has a story about this famous coat. Legendary Canadian singer/poet, Leonard Cohen, wrote in part, "…and those Montréal winters were bitter. I had this Red River Coat with a red sash and a toque with a pom pom and I was visible in the snow… she could see me from the kitchen window, but she never let me in." He refers to his mother leaving him out too long in the cold.

When Canada's renowned folk singer Gilles Vigneault wrote the song *"Mon pays ce n'est pas un pays, c'est l'hiver…"* (My country is not a country it's winter) he must have had Montréal in mind, as it seemed forever wrapped in a white mantle of snow. Montréal was home to Canada's Prime Minister Pierre Elliot Trudeau. He was born at 5779 rue Durocher in affluent Outremont, just one street over from our home on Hutchison Street. He frequented Parc Mont Royal as a child, and enjoyed it as much as we children did.

Hutchison Street ran smack dab into that spectacular mountain, which was within walking distance of Mont Royal. It was one of the most exhilarating downhill *glissades* that a little child could venture onto. Crisp packed snow "chunkled" underfoot as children trudged with their sleds and toboggans up the mountain. The rolling hills were speckled with colourful moving dots as children and adults alike enjoyed the hilarity of a sliding thrill. The cold crisp air bit at your cheeks as your breath created curly hot puffs in the tingling air.

There were little sleds that just fit your body as you steered with your legs and feet, and long padded toboggans that seated about ten people.

But the best sliding that we ever did was on a large flattened "Oxydol" cardboard soapbox! We'd sit on it and tightly grip the sides and "swoosh" down the mountain side and snowball past all the store bought sleighs and fancy toboggans, over bumps and knolls and up the bank to Park Avenue. Sometimes you travelled so fast that if you fell off your cardboard you'd still keep on going! If someone was in the way you just yelled, "Track…

track!" What the significance of that meant is beyond me, but everyone scattered. Besides being economical, you didn't have to drag it all the way home!

When we children weren't sliding or vying for marbles, we skated. Most of the time, we skated on the streets, which would be unthinkable today. But these were the post-war years; cars were at a premium and gas was rationed, so there were very few dangers to contend with. The milkman, bread man, and "Dusseault's Grocery Deliveries" all had horse-drawn sleighs, and we hitched many a ride on the backs of the carts much to the chagrin of the driver who constantly yelled, "*Arrêtez, maudit fouls.*" (Stop, damn fools.)

**MARGUERITE (MAGGIE) AND DOUGLAS IN MY RESIZED
RED RIVER COAT, TOQUE AND MITTS**

Hockey was another sport the boys played in the streets. My brother Johnny was obsessed with the Montréal Canadiens as were many other little boys. I think he even wore his red and blue "Hab" sweater to bed! My girlfriend Dee Dee's dad, Ray Getleff, wore Number 11 for the Montréal Canadiens from 1940-1945. Since he lived down the street from us, the boys used any excuse to go over to chat with Ray, who was more than obliging to give them tips on professional hockey. He was no Maurice Richard or Jean Béliveau, but then again who was?

On Querbes Street, in Outremont, was a beautiful park with an artificial pond that was reserved for skating on weekends. For ten cents we skated to the scratchy strains of "Blue Danube", and the ever popular "Lavender Blue, Dilly-Dilly, Lavender Green." Every little girl envisioned herself as Barbara Ann Scott as she cut figure eights on her "fancy" skates, as they were referred to in the 1940s.

Winter brought many games with it. Marbles was one of my favourites. It was an early spring pastime in many other provinces but it was *au contraire* in Québec. The first fall of fresh snow brought out our "Smokies" as we called them. We'd all run to Cousineau's on Bernard Street for a vast selection of multi-swirled "Cat's Eye", "Doubles" and "Kingers." My mother remembered them as being called "Knockers" back East and they were made of red clay. She would make us each a drawstring bag out of scraps of pretty flannelette and we'd fill them full of "Allies" as some kids called them, and it was off to see who could amass the most at the end of the day.

My friend Mo and I had many a scrap over marbles. There was quite a formality in preparing for the game. First we'd eye our boots, and when we both agreed who had the best heel, we'd round off a medium-sized hole in the snow. Then and only then would we proceed. Mo dented while I smoothed. We both stood five feet from the hole and threw closest to sinking the hole. "One potato, two potato, three potato, four, five potato, six potato, seven potato, more. I'm it! I'm first!" I said jumping up and down. We got testy at times. A call of "no fair, cheating" was heard more than once: "That's not in–", "Is too!" Now I know where the term "taking all your marbles and going home" came from!

As we walked home, clutching our flannelette bags, we stopped at Abie's candy store on the corner of St. Viateur Street for penny candy. We eyed the sweets in the glass oak case. There were large cherry wax lips, chocolate-covered "honeymoons", licorice pipes, syrup filled fudge cones, huge coconut balls, and jelly babies. For five pennies we had a large bag full. Soon we were skipping and sliding, arms around each other till we reached Hutchison Street. Mo headed for Park Avenue. "See you tomorrow, Jen," she called out waving a wet mitt. I ran back to her – "Last touch!" – I giggled as large snowflakes gently fell, covering our traces…

NOTRE-DAME

"It's early 1942, and we are still at war with Germany, remember that the prayers of little children reach our Heavenly Father first, so offer your commencement prayers for the souls of the dearly departed soldiers overseas," Sister Eulalia said.

The classroom of well behaved little soldiers of Christ, bowed their heads and prayed. "Hail Mary full of grapes, the Lord is with thee." We then stood smartly to attention next to the Union Jack and sang, "God Save the King," followed by "The Maple Leaf Forever."

This was École Notre-Dame de Bon Secours, a parochial bilingual Catholic school on Querbes Street in Outremont. The good Sisters of the Holy Names of Jesus and Mary ran the school. This was my first formal introduction to the English language.

We all wore compulsory uniforms of black worsted wool that itched constantly. The razor sharp pleats made us sit upright like miniature nuns. Starched high lace collars dug under tender little chins leaving a perpetual red line (suffering in silence assured you of a better spot in heaven). The ribbed cotton stockings were held in place with Coates half-inch elastic (tied in a knot), which restricted normal blood flow and accounted for blue feet most of the time!

Completing the outfit, were heavy fleece-lined navy blue bloomers down to mid-thigh, and more elastic. "We mustn't let little boys get impure thoughts," the holy nuns reminded us.

A large "Scapular" medal the size of a fifty-cent piece, of Jesus, Mary and Joseph was held in place with a large safety pin on our woolen undershirt. *If the Germans ever come to Montréal, I am well protected,* I thought.

Notre-Dame was all spit and polish. The grounds were meticulously kept and the halls shone brilliantly from the reflection of the hallowed halos of forty nuns. We children had the belief that nuns were not born, they just always "were".

There was the daily Catechism, recitation of the Rosary and the basic three "R's". Then there was the preoccupation with sin. There was original sin, mortal sin, venial sin, the seven deadly sins, and sins of omission.

When we weren't learning about sin, we were offering up indulgences for those who had! We were forever on our knees. While we squirmed and sometimes lost our balance, the nuns knelt as rigid as the holy statues that graced our desks.

The Sisters had little wooden "klackers", which were two pieces of wood hinged together and hollowed in the centre that produced a deafening "klack" when banged together. Sister Eulalia had a penchant for them and never missed her target when she had you in range. If she left you with a bump, you were to offer it up for the poor souls in purgatory. *Let them get their own bumps,* I thought angrily. This was definitely not a place for crybabies!

While passing a nun in the hallways, we were to practice humility and cast our eyes down, genuflect, and repeat an ejaculation of "Jesus, Mary and Joseph." We didn't know why, but we just did it.

Not this time, I thought rubbing my bump. *I'm not gonna look down, in fact, I'm not even gonna genuflect.* Bad choice!

I was abruptly pulled up to the face of this short little nun, who was not much taller than I. It was Sister Eulalia. Her nose almost touching mine, made me notice two long hairs growing out of her chin. *Wow! Nuns have hair,* I thought. Time was of the essence as Sister grabbed me by the ear and "klacked" me off to Mother Superior's office for a good lesson in humility.

All the way I stifled a cry, not for my burning ear, which was now fastened firmly between Sister Eulalia's fingers, but for my soul, which was surely damned to the fires of hell for provoking one of God's supernatural beings.

I was pushed into a small waiting room, for "the big one" – Mother Superior. Through my tears I surveyed my surroundings. The walls were a chalk white, no, more like a holy white. The large stark windows sparkled. The corners of the panes had been diligently cleaned out with orange sticks, as an act of penance for young novitiates.

A spindly wood table in the corner looked too fragile to hold the large marble bowl of holy water, stained with a yellow residue. A large crucifix hung in the centre of the wall depicting Christ's agony on the cross. His blood oozed brightly, *like real blood*, I thought. I shivered and lowered my eyes where they rested on the green linoleum floor. It was clean and shining. My mind wandered. *I wonder if they use Johnson paste wax on the floor like our house, and do they all get together when no one is looking and put wool socks over their stubby shoes, and skate this floor to a diamond-like shine.* Somehow the thought of a flock of nuns slipping and sliding, their billowing black skirts falling over their heads like a bunch of penguins sliding on the ice made me laugh to myself. I bit my tongue in penance, *Mea culpa, mea culpa, mea maxima culpa. That should do it,* I thought.

Silently, Mother Superior entered the room, only the rustle of her black skirts announced her presence. *I'm doomed*, I thought. "Jesus, Mary and Joseph," I said as I skirted a deep genuflect.

"Now, what is it that Jeannette did that was so bad?" she asked. The softness in the way she addressed me moved me to tears. "God loves you little Jeannette you did nothing serious wrong, perhaps bent things a little, but that can be remedied."

"Are you one of God's angels?" I asked.

She laughed out loud. "We are far from being angels my child, we make mistakes too. Can you keep a secret?" she whispered. "When I was a little girl like you, I stole a nickel that didn't belong to me."

"You did?" I said, my eyes widening. *Wow, a stealing nun, wait till I tell Pezzie,* I thought.

"Now, off you go, wash your face and follow me to the kitchen. The Sisters are in the midst of candy making for the church bazaar, and if you won't think too harshly of Sister Eulalia, you may have a cinnamon lollipop."

I smiled meekly but my earache did not have the same sentiment.

Months had passed when Mother Superior came to our classroom and announced sadly that we were to pray for the soul of our dearly departed Sister Eulalia, who was now resting in the arms of Jesus. It was so much better than saying that she had "died" or something similar. She made it sound like she floated to heaven without passing "Go".

Some of the children cried, but I felt the recent bump on the side of my head and wondered if there is justice on this earth like the nuns say, was God reprimanding her up there… maybe He's making her genuflect over and over to a high archangel somewhere.

Kneel… klack. Stand… klack… Silence… klack–klack – twice on the head, I thought. *I wonder… naw, God wouldn't do that… or would He?*

As a child in Montréal, my heart would race with pure joy when I was at the centre of my favourite street, Park Avenue. There were clanging streetcars, people bustling about, and shoppers everywhere. Children were to be seen and not heard in those days, so it was easy to meld blissfully into the fray of childhood fantasy.

On Friday after school, Pezzie, my fourth grade school chum and I, would hold hands and hop-and-skip all over Park Avenue. She had a cute "Maggie Muggins" doll face with a sprinkling of freckles that dotted the tip of her nose, which ran down to her impish grin.

First, we'd peer into Mr. Levine's bakery window savoring all those sweet delectable pastries. There were lemon butterfly cupcakes, chocolate éclairs, flaky Napoleons, gooey jelly doughnuts and hundreds of petit fours.

Deliberately pressing our noses to the clean window always prompted the baker to come running out and scold us, but not before he bribed us with the usual cookie!

Chewing on our cookie, we made our way past the Metropolitan to the Woolworth's 5 and 10 cents store and past the Rialto Theatre. Across the street, was "Benny's", Montréal's famous smoked meat restaurant on Park Avenue (not to be confused with "Ben's" restaurant in downtown Montréal). Benny's opened in 1908. You could buy a huge smoked meat sandwich and French fries for twenty-five cents.

There, if we stood on our tippy toes, we would be eye level to huge moist chunks of the most delicious meat in the world. Inhaling deeply, the intoxicating aroma of special spices caressed our nostrils. We gazed at the peppercorns that floated over the steaming juices.

Our eyes transfixed as we watched the cook in his grease-splattered apron prepare an ordered sandwich. Scooping up a hot chunk of steaming meat, he plopped it firmly onto a juice-soaked board, sending bits of juice to splatter on the window. With the skill of a surgeon, he proceeded to slice the meat into paper-thin layers that fell gently onto steaming pink piles, to the waiting thick slice of Jewish rye bread. This gastronomic sight proved too much for me as I turned to Pezzie and said, "When I grow up I'm gonna buy a big chunk of meat just like that and eat it all by myself"… and I did!

But as time went on and I could explore the many *charcuteries* this city could offer, I came across the famous one and only smoked meat restaurant that Montréal had to offer. It is a small little nook tucked away on Boulevard Saint-Laurent, known as "the Main" in downtown Montréal. Enter…Schwartz's. The sign says it all: Montréal's Hebrew Delicatessen founded in 1928. If by chance you can't find it, just follow the long lines of patient patrons who are enticed by the intoxicating aromas, of steaming spiced brisket and French fries. Schwartz's, a place immortalized in the literature of none other than Mordecai Richler. Many political deals were hashed out on those wooden tables. It is a place to see and be seen. It saw its share of celebrities throughout the decades. Alas, as the old saying goes "all good things come to an end."

In 2012, an announcement in the Montreal Gazette stated that Schwartz's was closing… a death knell to Montréalers. However, a very famous Québecer came to the rescue!

Canadian singer Celine Dion and husband René Angélil have since purchased Schwartz's. The couple has promised to preserve the integrity and history of this beautiful diamond in the rough. Montréal will be pleased. Merci, Celine!

In the 1940s, Good Friday (*Vendredi Saint*) for Roman Catholics was a Holy Day of obligation and meant one must abstain from eating meat as a small remembrance of Christ's sacrifice. Catholics were under the pain of mortal sin if you so much as sniffed at a hamburger! Not that there was an abundance of that either. Our elders were constantly telling us that we were at war and that we were fortunate that we could still afford Mr. Shapiro's two for twenty-five cents salt herring.

"*Demain, c'est Vendredi Saint* and it's your turn to go to Steinberg's," my mother said, switching from French to English. "Give me twenty-five cents wort' of sugar and don' forget the ration book dis time."

For eight cents, you could buy ten pounds of potatoes, for ten cents, a loaf of bread and another ten cents, a glass bottle of milk with three inches of cream rising to the top, capped with a neat cardboard stopper.

I skipped down from Park Avenue to St. Viateur Street, where Mr. Shapiro's little old-fashioned grocery store was. There were plucked naked chickens hanging by their necks on strings in the window and fresh vegetables and fruit piled high in wooden bins out front. I loved the wonderful pungent aroma that filled my nostrils; it was so Jewish, I thought. There were kosher dill pickles in huge wooden kegs, fresh baked rye breads, braided Challah, knishes, halva in shiny square tins, and hard bagels threaded on ropes.

I was a curious child and even at this early age loved food. My eye caught the tall pickling barrel. I stood there tracing the metal strapping with my finger, wanting to lift the wooden lid and smell the tangy aroma of salt herring. I thought they looked like the drawing of the loaves and fishes in my Catechism book.

Mr. Shapiro, a kindly old man, always bundled in layers of old cardigans even in summer, leaned on his worn counter. He surveyed me quizzically through his bifocals. (I didn't have a quarter and he knew it).

"Just browsing," I said before he had a chance to ask.

"No quarter today?"

"No money," I shrugged.

"Money… shmoney… vot's money?" he asked as he lifted the salt encrusted lid, took out two fat silver kosher herring and laid them on the Montreal Star newspaper. He wrapped them tightly in a sheet of newspaper and tied it with butcher string in a tight bow. "Here, little one, for your Mammilla. Happy Good Friday."

"Herring for no money?" I squealed.

"No money," he smiled.

"Thank you so much, Mr. Shapiro."

"Mazel Tov," he answered.

I can't believe that he gave me two herring for no money, maybe they will multiply by the time I get home, I thought.

Armed with my free herring, I ran down the lane as fast as my little legs would carry me. *I can hardly wait to tell everyone — all except the Happy Good Friday part,* I thought excitedly.

It's Friday and Mom usually waxes the long halls. The following day, we children would don old woolen socks and skate the long narrow corridor to a brilliant shine. The clean smell of Johnson's floor wax mingled with the aroma of fresh homemade bread, ragout and baked beans signaled that all was right in our world. With mounting excitement, I flung the back door open my eyes open wide. The assault on my nostrils was gripping, and stopped me in my tracks.

"What is that disgusting smell?" I asked.

There was the culprit, my father, sitting at the kitchen table, a (seemingly) pile of burnt sticks on a plate set before him and a look of sheer ecstasy on his face. He was chewing and grinning as if he took pleasure in offending us with this odour. It was our penalty for not knowing that heating smoked Caplin (a small silvery fish) on a bare stovetop is a Newfoundlander's delight! He then proceeded to teach us mainlanders on the elaborate and mysterious reproduction of the tasty little Capelin and the many ways of cooking them (the stovetop method is not recommended!).

Somehow, with all this commotion, my free herring, which had now soaked through the newspaper, was creating a stink of its own. Somehow, it didn't seem to matter as I had other things on my mind like: I wonder if God minded that we ate kosher herring that was blessed by a Jewish rabbi on a Roman Catholic's Good Friday? Oy vey!

EASTER IN MONTRÉAL

Montréal was like a Phoenix rising from the ashes of a cold grey winter. The war was ending, it was spring, and Easter was just around the corner. We were thankful to be alive! Windows were left wide open, so as to breathe the fresh air into homes after the long cold winter.

Radios blared loudly from every house, the Andrews Sisters singing "Don't sit under the apple tree, with anyone else but me, till I come marching home!" … and "Why do girls prefer this way to relieve the distress of female weakness? Use Lady E Pinkham vegetable compound."

"And now it's time for the Happy Gang! So if you're happy and healthy, the heck with being wealthy, and keep happy with the Happy Gang! Tune in tomorrow morning at 11:15 for Ma Perkins, brought to you by, 'Rinso'."

JEANNETTE DOUGIE, MARGUERITE BILLY AND BOBBY

Mrs. Rosenberg's rugs are all pegged neatly on the line. Their bulky weight strains them down as she beats the winter's dust out of them. Swat… swat… swat, keeping in time to the children skipping chants.

> *"Ice cream soda lemonade tart;*
> *tell me the name of your sweetheart."*
>
> *"I see England, I see France,*
> *I see a hole in Monique's pants."*
>
> *"Whistle while you work, Mussolini lost his shirt.*
> *Hitler wore it, Britain tore it, whistle while you work."*

"One, two, three, a Laree.
My first name is Mary,
If you think it's necessary,
Look it up in the dictionary."

My mother and your mother were hanging out the clothes
My mother gave your mother a punch in the nose
What colour was the blood?
Blue…B…L…U…E spells BLUE
and out goes Y…O…U!

Sidewalks were swept clean for hopscotch. They were also perfect for writing messages like Kilroy was here. Mo hates Peter's guts! Moiche eats worms!

Roller skates were dug out of closets. It made one feel important as you dangled your skate key on an old string around your neck, and you also hoped your mother wouldn't notice the gouge it left on your leather-soled shoes as you tightened the key to its limit.

"Bolo" bats were always breaking their elastics, and "yo-yos their string, and every little girl had a "Cross" ball.

A sure sign of spring was when the crate scooters appeared racing down the street, (a version of today's skateboard with an orange crate nailed to one end). They were decorated with pennants and brightly coloured stickers. My brothers Billy and Bobby always had the best ones on the block. They even improvised working night-lights, by ingeniously inserting a candle in an old empty tomato can!

There were flowers everywhere. The butchers inserted purple and yellow paper curls amid the pork chops and hamburger. The *vitrines* on Park Avenue were festooned with daffodils and pink bunny rabbit cutouts. Delivery boys decorated their three-wheel box bicycles with brightly coloured crêpe paper, and when in motion produced a kaleidoscope of bright colours.

Every horse had an Easter hat! Borden's and JJ Joubert milk companies seem to hold their own horse bonnet parade!

Woolworth's 5 and 10 cent store sold hat forms for twenty-five cents each. Ladies would decorate them with birds and flowers, and bits of ribbon, the more elaborate the better. St. Michael's church was ablaze with colour on Easter morn.

The day before Easter we all gathered round the kitchen table and excitedly prepared for the traditional egg painting, a welcomed relief from the gloomy church rituals and obligatory physical denials that we endured. "For forty days and forty nights" we wailed loudly to anyone who listened.

My mother taught us to decorate Easter eggs by dipping coloured crêpe paper in hot water and patiently colouring the eggs to create our own individual masterpieces. We also use beet juice to produce magenta and ruby coloured eggs. She also showed me how her mother had a unique way of colouring Easter eggs at home in New Brunswick. She did this using onionskins; she took all the dried brown skins and boiled them until the water turned light amber. She then gently dropped the eggs and simmered them to a golden henna shade.

"Hot cross buns, one a penny, two a penny, hot cross buns," we all chanted round the table. I thought my mother's recipe was the best in the whole world, light and golden with thick iced crosses on top and lots of cinnamon. According to old Acadian folklore, a good batch of hot cross buns on Easter ensured successful baking all year.

As we all gathered around the kitchen table my father gave the blessing. "Bless us O Lord and these gifts which we are about to receive from thy bounty through Christ our Lord, Amen." Easter was now in full swing, no more penance, no more confessions and best of all, no more fasting!

MOM'S HOT CROSS BUNS

The potato in this recipe is what makes it a light "cross bun". During the war, people used lard or shortening instead of butter and there was no instant yeast either. I have substituted the cake yeast for the "traditional" style granulated yeast in packages. Make sure that you measure the yeast.

½ cup mashed potatoes	1 egg well beaten
½ cup milk	1 tbsp "traditional" rising yeast
½ cup water	¼ cup lukewarm water
¼ cup butter	3 cups sifted unbleached flour
5 tbsp sugar	1 tsp sugar
1 tsp salt	2 tbsp cinnamon
1 cup mixed candied peel & fruit	½ tsp allspice
½ cup raisins	⅛ tsp clove

Combine potatoes, milk, water, butter, sugar and salt. Stir and heat until butter melts. Remove from heat and cool to lukewarm. Transfer to a large bowl.

Dissolve 1 tsp sugar into the warm water, sprinkle the yeast on it and let it set for about 10 minutes until it is foamy. Stir 1 cup of the sifted flour, cinnamon allspice and cloves into the potato mixture. Stir the foamy yeast mixture and add egg and fruits. Stir in remaining flour to make a soft dough.

Let stand for five minutes, then knead until soft and satiny, adding flour gradually using your hands to mix the dough, add more flour if needed (don't make the dough too stiff, as it will result in a harder bun). Place in an oiled bowl. Cover with a clean cloth. Let rise for about an hour, or when doubled in bulk.

Punch down and form 12 buns of equal size on a greased cookie sheet with enough space for them to expand. With a sharp knife, slit a cross on tops and cover with a cloth. Let rise until double in bulk. Brush with beaten egg and bake at 400°F 15-20 minutes until golden brown. Decorate with frosted crosses.

FROSTING

1 cup icing sugar	milk
½ tsp vanilla	

Add milk and vanilla to the icing sugar slowly, until desired consistency. Pipe on warm buns.

THE SUKKAH

Two weeks after the Jewish New Year, and five days after Yom Kippur, a little makeshift wooden hut would appear in our neighbour's backyard almost overnight.

The morning sun filters through the trees, casting silver glints on Mr. Rosenberg's snowy white beard as he slowly covers his hut with leaves. He is a simple and holy man, and is celebrating Sukkah, the feast of Tabernacles. He will live in this hut for seven days.

> *"You shall dwell in booths seven days; all that are home born in Israel shall dwell in booths; that your generations may know that I made the children of Israel to dwell in booths, when I brought them out of the land of Egypt."*
>
> —*Leviticus 23: 33-44*

He is distracted for a moment by Mrs. Rosenberg, who surveys all this from her kitchen window. Wiping her hands on her apron, and with quick short steps, crosses the yard to where he is standing. She proceeds to rearrange the leaves on the side of the heart. He looks at her distastefully, like he is thinking, *How can she do this? This is my hut*. An argument ensues.

"Stop this, this is my hut."

"You stop already, the Gentiles are watching." Sara continues, ignoring his pleas. (This by the way is all in Yiddish, and the above is my childish interpretation.)

The Yiddish bickering goes on. "Oy vey," he says throwing his hands up in despair, and wonders why God in all his wisdom has made woman especially this one so stubborn.

Nevertheless they loved each other dearly, and when the Gentiles weren't looking, she would stroke his soft white beard affectionately and with a sigh, his arm would wrap gently around the small of her back.

> *To dwell in the Sukkah is punishment enough. To have one's wife in a Sukkah for seven days would be an additional punishment.*
>
> —*Jewish saying*

Hanukah was a fun time for our Jewish friends. It was very close to our Christmas, so we shared gifts, as kids often do, we didn't mind, as they seem to have more than we did. Each child received the traditional dreidel, a spinning top. Whoever spins it longest gets to choose their favourite sweet. Sometimes the dreidels were made of silver and filled with money. They used to ask us "what is it that has one foot and cannot stand, but can dance?" A Hanukkah, dreidel of course.

As most religions, they celebrated with food. I have yet found anyone's recipe that could compare with Mrs. Rosenberg's cheese blintzes.

It reminded me of the story of when this kind householder, who after the morning services at the synagogue, invited a stranger to his home for the festival meal, and a taste of his wife's cooking. It was a custom for the hostess to serve cheese blintzes.

"I see that you enjoyed my blintzes, here have another," the wife urged.

"Yes, I certainly did, however I don't want to deprive you of any more."

"You've eaten six already," she reminded him, "but then again who's counting?"

CHEESE BLINTZES

CRÊPES

1 cup sifted all-purpose
flour
5 tsp sugar
4 eggs

1 cup milk
1 cup water
shortening or clarified butter

Sift flour with sugar. Beat the eggs, and add them to the dry ingredients. Beat mixture until smooth. It should have the consistency of heavy cream. Set the batter to one side for 30 minutes. If batter becomes too thick, a spoonful of water may be added.

Heat a 10-inch frying pan to smoking temperature, grease lightly with shortening or clarified butter. Pour about two tablespoonful of batter on hot pan. Remove from heat and swirl and rotate pan to form a thin crêpe. Return pan to the heat and rotate it quickly. The crêpes are done when the middle is set and the bottom is golden brown. Lift the edges of the crêpe and turn over. Do not overcook.

Keep crêpes warm in a slow oven 200°F, or stack them between waxed paper and store in the freezer (if not using right away). Prepared crêpes may also be found in the frozen food section of your grocer.

BLINTZ FILLING

1 lb cottage cheese	½ tsp vanilla
2 large egg yolks	¼ cup sour cream
(well beaten)	1½ tbsp sugar

For added taste, I add 1 tsp finely grated orange zest.

Cream cottage cheese until very smooth and creamy. Add egg yolks, vanilla, sour cream and sugar. Salt to taste. Mix thoroughly. Set aside.

Place heaping tablespoon of cheese filling into centre of pancake. Fold one side down, then the other. Then fold over the ends. Place on a cookie sheet. Bake for 20 minutes at 350°F until golden brown.

Serve warm or cold with sour cream and applesauce, or my favourite, strawberries and Grande Marnier! Makes about 16 blintzes.

✑ THE PROTESTANTS ✑

Every second Saturday would find my friend Maureen and I sitting on the sidewalk curb watching the Montréal Public Works Dept. We sat patiently waiting while the men lowered long-handled scoops down the drain, hauling up debris of dead leaves, papers and slimy guck! If we were lucky we'd be the recipient of another little girl's folly, a perfectly good used "Cross" ball. Then we would run home and soak it in *eau de*

Javel (bleach) for an hour, and then it was off to bounce merrily away, "One... Two... Three... Alaree."

Not this time though, as we watched the dripping scoop overflowing with soggy maple leaves with nary a ball in sight. *"À la prochaine,"* (until next time) the workmen waved as they continued on to Bernard Street. As we sat glumly with our hands under our chins, we contemplated our next move.

"I know what," I said with excitement. "Let's go see what the Protestants are doing today," I nudged at Mo.

"Yeah, let's go! This is the day they serve all those pretty cakes and things," she said excitedly.

Being a Protestant must be a cinch, we thought, as it meant no penance, no kneeling, no confessing, no fasting before communion, nor saving pennies for Chinese pagan babies. And besides being rich, all they ever did in church was to sit or sing. And boy did they sing! You could hear them all the way down the back lane.

"Alleluia... Alleluia... Alleluia." Even Rabbi Mendelssohn unconsciously kept time on his prayer book as he waited out front for the Rosemont Tramway.

We ran down to the Presbyterian Church on Park Ave. and jimmied the back window and leaned in up to our waists. Our mouths drooled at the sight of all those goodies that were prepared for the congregation. "Wonder where they got all the ration coupons for all that sugar."

"Gee, Protestants are rich aren't they? Look at all that chocolate icing," Mo said smacking her lips.

"Which one would you eat if you had a chance?" I asked.

"This one, and this one, and this one, and that one," she pointed out as she strained towards the cakes, and with that she dropped her Cross ball on the table with a crash. We watched in disbelief as it uncontrollably plopped from cake to cake.

"Let's get out of here fast," I said. But Maureen wasn't about to lose her best Cross ball, so she edged herself inside only to be aided by the strong hand of the minister who promptly inquired about which church we attended.

"We're Protestants," Mo piped up.

"Protestants!" I hissed grabbing her sweater. "Are you crazy? Do you want us to go to hell?"

"Shush and cross your fingers," she whispered.

"Yup, we're Protestants" she insisted, pointing to the both of us.

"And what about you, young lady?" he asked (young lady meant the jig was up).

"Yup, I'm protestant too," I said as I stared nonchalantly at the scab on my knee.

"Well children, I guess if you're really Protestants I can do nothing else but invite you into the House of God."

"The House of God, sheesh!" Mo said. "This is just a basement."

"And perhaps after lunch you can lead us into our next song – Yes Jesus loves me, the bible tells me so – every little Protestant girl knows that one," he said with a wink.

"We don't know that song Mo, that's Prespetation or something. What are we going to do?"

"Just move your lips," she said smiling, as she retrieved her gooey ball, wiping it on the bottom of her dirndl skirt. "And be happy it's not in Hebrew."

As the Reverend Atkins walked away I heard him call out, "Set two more places for a couple of Micks from St. Michael's parish."

"What's a 'Mick', Mo?" I asked.

"Who cares," she said as she stuffed her face with a mille-feuille or Napoléon, which squirted custard all down her chin. The brownie that I bit into stuck dryly in my throat. Now, how was I ever going to confess to Father Kelly that I was a Protestant for a day and a "Mick" to boot!

Afterwards, we slowly made our way back home with our singsong "We are Protestants, We are Protestants." Just before turning down my street, Mo yelled out "Jeannette is going to hell-ell", which then made me laugh. I ran back to her – "Last touch."

NOËL IN MONTRÉAL DURING THE WAR YEARS

The Eaton's catalogue played a large part of the preparation for Christmas in many Canadian homes. That's the time of the year when every mother stretched the already thin dollar to miraculous lengths.

As a family, we sat around the kitchen table and spread the glossy coloured pages of the proverbial "Wish" book. There were pretty Eaton's "beauty" dolls with porcelain faces with rosebud lips; high-buttoned shoes for little girls; and, fancy high-heeled figure skates with "Barbara Ann Scott" imprinted on them.

My mother longingly traced the outline of a pretty lace dress, while my little brothers tugged impatiently at the boy's section and the Montréal Canadiens sweaters, hockey sticks, skates and sleds.

This time of year brought with it bittersweet feelings for my mother, as she knew the glossy pictures were the closest she'd ever get to the real thing.

A must with every Eaton's order, were sealed "Treasure" boxes that could be had for one dollar. We could hardly contain ourselves when we opened the surprise. In it you were sure to find spools of coloured thread, odd buttons, colouring books, bits of ribbon, "ball and Jacks," a "bolo" bat, and perhaps a tin whistle. Once I got a celluloid Kewpie doll with real feathers for hair and sparkles in her bellybutton!

In mid-November, St. Catherine Street was alive with children in anticipation of the annual Santa Clause parade. Santa was the finest, with a splendid suit of deep scarlet and flowing gossamer beard. He remains in a special place in my heart to this very day!

After the parade, we all amassed at Eaton's Toy Ville for a ride on the mini electric trains. Standing on the noisy wooden escalators that shook and rattled all the way to the fifth floor, our hearts beat faster as our necks craned from side to side so as not to miss a single thing. The strains of the "toot-toot" of the train and the loud jingle of bells as we neared Magic Land were exhilarating. We knew the electric train was waiting to take us through magical Toy Ville. At the end of the line, each flush-cheeked child received a wrapped Christmas gift.

In 1948, the debut of "Punkinhead", Eaton's beloved stuffed bear, was prominently displayed on mounds of toys.

Our journey would not be complete without viewing Eaton's mechanical Christmas window display. Little noses pressed to cold windows and freezing feet did not deter our excitement. Charles Dickens' "Tiny Tim" came alive and hobbled on crutches. There were prancing reindeer, regal marching nutcrackers, dolls that touched their toes, dancing snowmen and an array of glittering gifts. We stood transfixed… there were no words, just mindful dancing of sugarplums, and that enchanting fairy dust called Eaton's Department store at Christmas time!

It was the post-war depression, many families went without; we were fortunate in that my father, a mechanical engineer, was employed by the Dominion Engineering Company in Montréal and was somewhat secure. He was sent however for two years to Venezuela, in South America, where he was responsible for testing and installing power plants for the class "J" minesweepers. My mother on the other hand had the challenge of bringing up a large family all alone. The monthly paycheques were at times haphazardly late, due to the extreme disruption in postal services attributed to the war and this time was one of them.

One Christmas that will always stay close to my heart was the Christmas when there was no tree.

"No tree?" my baby brother asked.

"*Non, mon petit bebé.*"

Not only was there no tree, but no presents either. Children have a way of blocking out bad news, so we went on as usual knowing that Santa would never let us down.

Christmas Eve was upon us; the city was deluged with a heavy fall of fresh snow. Across the street the darkened living room of our neighbour's house accented the twinkling of the bright-hued lights on a towering Christmas tree. There were two silhouettes of a husband and wife as they shared the holiday spirit together and waved a friendly "hello".

My mother was silent in her thoughts. If she cried, she never showed it. It was early evening and we were silently preparing supper when, all of a sudden the front door opened wide. Frigid cold air tunneled up the long narrow hall to our warm feet. Wafting behind it was the crisp green smell of fresh spruce boughs. Silently, we all ran towards it.

There on the floor, lay a very spindly tree with my little brother's hand proudly fastened tightly to its trunk.

"*Mon dieu*, a Christmas tree! Billy, where you get that?" my mother said happily.

"On Park Avenue. No one wanted it because it's too skinny, but we do don't we, Mom?" he said, his big blue eyes glowing.

CHRISTMAS ON HUTCHISON STREET 1945

"Oui, oui take it in de parlour near de window."

We bustled about dragging Christmas decorations out of the closet, laughing and singing while Mom swept the snow off of little Billy with the kitchen broom.

We filled the vacant spaces in our slim little tree with Christmas cards, made with my baby brother's drawings. After trimming the tree, we stood back in awe of the happy little tree that no one wanted and sang "O Little Town Of Bethlehem."

Now, it truly is Christmas, I thought.

Mom made us hot cocoa while we hung our stockings from the mantelpiece, half hoping that Santa would come, and after all, we did have a tree.

Christmas morning...We rushed to the living room and dumped our stockings on the floor. There was an orange, an apple, barley toy, and ribbon candy that stuck to the wool of the stocking. Under the tree was a pair of mittens for us all (made by cutting a mitten pattern out of the good part of a worn sweater, then embroidered around the edges with multicoloured wool). My mittens had little flowers on the front. I also got a rag doll, suspiciously made from the same material. Santa had come! No one complained, even though we only had chicken for Christmas dinner, we knew there were others less fortunate than us.

As we all sat huddled at the foot of our dear little tree, my mother pointed to the Christ child and reminded us what Christmas is really all about. As she hugged us all my little brother Johnny said, "This is the best Christmas ever."

And he was so right!

∽ MAPLE SYRUP ∾

The indigenous people of Canada discovered the food properties of maple sap long before the arrival of European settlers. The North American natives however first discovered how to extract the tree sap and called it *"sinzibukwud"*, which means, "drawn from wood." Canada is now the world's largest exporter of maple syrup.

Canada is synonymous with the red maple leaf. In 1734, the St. John the Baptist Society chose the maple leaf as its symbol. The maple leaf represents many Canadian institutions. The first Canadian coin minted with the maple leaf was the penny. In 1867, the song "The Maple Leaf Forever" was officially designated as Canada's Confederation song.

In 1965, under the direction of Prime Minister Lester B. Pearson, the red maple leaf that proudly unfurls today was inaugurated as the official flag of Canada.

During and after World War II, Canadians were encouraged to consume maple syrup instead of sugar, as it was much less expensive and not rationed; however, well guarded.

My fondest memory regarding maple syrup was in the modest kitchen of Mme Bernier. Mme Bernier was a family friend and fabulous cook. She was also, as the Québécois would say *pur laine,* which means "pure wool," which refers to people of original French Canadian ancestry. Mme Bernier lived on Park Avenue in a large flat with her four daughters.

On Saturdays, I would bounce my 'Cross' ball against their back door, in hopes of being noticed and invited in. Well, it never failed.

Mme Bernier's face would appear framed in the small lace-curtained window. "*Entrée, ma belle,*" she'd say, her hazel eyes twinkling while wiping her hands on her frilly pink apron.

The heat of the stove flushed her cheeks red like the little girl on the Campbell soup label. She had a coquettish look about her that was so endearing. The aroma of her kitchen was like a big warm hug. A large pot of meat sitting on the counter was probably for her delectable Québec *tourtière* no doubt.

"Sit… eer," she said patting the wooden chair with its flowered cotton backing. "I made *tarte au sirop d'érable*. You like some, *non?*" she said, practicing her English on me.

There on the cupboard sat a thick, rich, creamy, maple syrup pie. Next to it was a small bowl of whipped cream. My eyes widened, my mouth watered, I wanted a piece, *"Oui, s'il vous plaît,"* I answered.

She cut off a respectable slice, and scraping the bits, which clung to the side of the knife, slid it lovingly onto a pretty flowered plate. As the first forkful entered my mouth, I was in sweet maple heaven! At that moment I knew Mme Bernier would always have a special place in my heart.

Through the years, this age old maple syrup recipe was prepared and served on many of my *Reveillon* tables at Christmas. Countless requests for this coveted simple recipe are still in demand today. Mme Bernier's daughter Claire, kindly submitted two of her mother's famous recipes, which I inserted here for you the reader. This is a tribute to a wonderful lady, Madame Jeannette Bernier.

MADAME BERNIER'S MAPLE SYRUP PIE

This recipe is over 100 years old!

4 tbsp butter	½ cup whole milk (I use cream)
6 tbsp flour	1½ cups Canadian maple syrup

In a medium-sized saucepan, melt butter. Add flour and mix thoroughly. Remove from heat. Add milk or cream and the maple syrup. Stir well. Boil for 2-3 minutes. Cool, then pour into a cooked pie shell and decorate with whipped cream. I decorate mine with walnuts.

MADAME BERNIER'S TOURTIÈRE

Québec meat pie

During the war, Mrs. Bernier used to put her *tourtières* in the back shed (no refrigerators back then) for about a week before Christmas. It was a constant chore keeping the door closed to keep the alley cats from tasting her cooking.

1 lb ground pork (or ¾ Ib pork and ¼ lb ground beef)	¼ tsp allspice
	Salt and pepper to taste
1 small onion	1 small bay leaf
⅓ cup warm water	1 favourite double pie crust recipe

Sauté chopped onion, add meat and cook slowly until it loses its pink colour, (take care not to overcook!). Add warm water, spice, salt pepper and bay leaf. Cook a little longer. Remove bay leaf. Cool mixture before putting in pie crust. Cook at 325°F until golden.

"SEE SPAWT RUN"

Darkness descends early in Montréal as winter approaches. Shutters are drawn tight, as the family settles easily for the night. An old coal furnace warms the house. The hot water radiator hisses and rattles demanding another saucer to accommodate its spill.

My brother Johnny is huddled by the old Marconi radio, his ear glued to the speaker. The tips of his ears are as red as his Montréal Canadiens sweater, as he listens to the voice of Foster Hewitt: "Maurice Richard skates to the Maple Leaf net... he deeks... he shoots... he *scores!*"

"Did you hear that, Mom? He did it again!" he says rubbing his temples excitedly.

"That's nice, Johnny," Mom answered, as she had other things on her mind.

She sat at the kitchen table, her hair rolled under in a roll like "Rosie the Riveter" (the latest rage in the forties). Her face was flushed from the heat of the wood cook stove. In her hands was my little brother's grade two "Reader." With a look of determination in her eyes, she was diligently trying to teach herself to read English. (A difficult task since my father neither spoke nor understood French, nor had he the interest to do so!)

'See spot run,' she saw written in the book.

Jack & Maggie
Beaver lake Mount Royal
Montreal 1945

JACK & MARGUERITE (MAGGIE) 1945

"Cee... sput... ran. Cee... sput...ron," she drawls loudly. "Cee... spout... rawwnn," she slowly enunciates.

My father who was listening to all this, interjected, "It's not 'Sput' Margaret, it's 'Spot,' like 'Spaawwwt,'"as he drawled the 'awt.' If you're going to learn the English language, do it properly!"

"See spot run!" She turned her head slowly and stared at him in disbelief. "Oh, now, it's 'spawt' is it, monsieur? Spawt... spawt, well, I don' spawt a French book in your 'ands!" she said indignantly with her hands on her hips. "Stubborn English Newfoundlander, *tête dur*" (hard head), she muttered to herself.

My father's face reddened, but he managed a grin, as he knows she's right and admires her feistiness!

I always wondered how they ever communicated in the earlier years when they couldn't understand each other. My mother once said, "When I met your fadder, 'ee was so 'andsome and he learn me 'eenglish like; yes and no. After a while de no become yes and dat's ow it 'appends, love do funny tings to people," she said with a sly smile.

Many years have passed since that winter night in Montréal. My mother did eventually learn to speak English very well, but kept her melodic French accent.

When my father passed away, my mother visited his gravesite. There she found her stubborn "Jack" in a New Brunswick cemetery, flanked by two "Frenchmen" on either side. She affectionately smiled and wondered mischievously if he really knew what kind of "Spawt" he was in!

ST. JOSEPH

"Here it comes! Here it comes!" Maureen, who I nicknamed Mo, squealed as we stood at the tram stop on Park Avenue. It was a warm sunny morning and before us glistened the most glorious, golden chariot we'd ever seen... Montréal's open air observation streetcar. It had gold coloured iron grillwork and was festooned with coloured lamps and tiered seats.

Clang! Clang! The conductor pulls the cord. "All ab-o-a-r-rrd!" he shouts, as he helps us up the wide steps. Mo and I were off on a Saturday morning adventure. We had money to spend, fifty cents each to be exact (which was a lot of money for ten-year-olds). We made that money by selling ten books of tickets for the Catholic Federated Charities. For every book we sold, we were allowed to keep ten cents. Between us we made one whole dollar! It cost twenty cents return to tour from Park Avenue to Mount Royal, St. Catherine, Côte-des-Neiges and Parc Lafontaine. So that meant we had plenty left for a Mello-Roll ice cream cone.

We "clanged" down St. Catherine Street passing the big department stores of Eaton's, Henry Morgan's, Ogilvy's, Dupuis Frères, Woolworth's and Kresge's 5 and 10 cent store and the Montréal Forum.

Our necks craned from side to side as we read advertising signs like: "Castoria... the Dionne Quintuplets cry for It"... "Buy Victory Bonds"... "Veronica Lake has a 'Romance' Complexion"... Buy Pencil Seam "Phantom" Nylons...!" "I love a Man in an Adam's Hat"... *patates frites ...chiens chauds.*

Theatre headlines read Marlene Dietrich in "Kismet" with a cast of thousands. We especially liked the restaurant sign that sold Wimpey's Hamburger. It had a huge funny paper cartoon of "Wimpey", with his brush mustache gobbling down a giant burger.

Our noses reddened in the afternoon sun, so we decided to get off at the next stop and visit St. Joseph's Oratory. This basilica is dedicated to St. Joseph where Brother André is credited for his miraculous healings. Pope John Paul II beatified Brother André in 1982. Pope Benedict XVI later canonized the saint in 2010. Actually we were anxious to see if Brother André's heart, which was pickled in vinegar or something, was still there. It was encased in glass and the faithful would file past, touching it and praying for special favours. It looked pretty gross to us.

Montreal's Observation Car Built in 1924

Photograph taken in the 1950s By Frank Rossano of the CTM Volunteer staff.

OBSERVATION CAR

After running up the long trek of hundreds of stairs, and irreverently passing the humble praying on every step, we reached the Oratory's vestibule. We were distracted for a moment by a rather large statue of St. Joseph with his hands outstretched in a beckoning pose. He was covered in crimson lipstick smudges, which the faithful had bent to kiss in reverence. With hands on knees, we scrutinized the plaster likeness of the saint. "I bet we could do better than that," Mo said as she reached in her pinafore pocket and took out her red "Tangee" lipstick, which she had snitched from her aunt. We opened our mouths, pursed our lips in a big "0" and traced an outline on our lips like Clara Bow. We giggled as Mo went beyond her lips almost touching her nose. "There, now let's kiss St. Joseph!"

We kissed his nose, his hands, and even the plaster chip on the back of his head! When we got bored with all that kissing and bending, we stood back to view our handiwork. We both stood silent for a moment and thought to ourselves that this was not such a good idea after all.

Suddenly out of nowhere, a priest descended upon us, grabbing us both by the arms and started violently shaking us. All the while shouting a litany of atrocities that would befall on us: "You made Mother Mary cry, you know the punishment for that...You vile and wicked children, you will have to confess your sin for defacing church property!"

"Sheesh, it's only a statue," Mo wailed.

"We'd better get out of here before he turns us into a pillar of salt," I said.

We thought we were home free until we heard his parting shouts of, "Just think of all the germs that you've spread, and God knows how many you picked up!" We both froze in our tracks.

I said, "What if we get polio or something?"

Mo groaned, "I don't feel so good."

"Me neither," I chimed, "my throat is kinda sore."

"Serves us right, now we're both gonna die," added Mo.

The long drive home was silent as we examined our consciences. We didn't even stop for our Mello-Roll. As we got off the tram on Park Avenue with the webbed imprint of the straw seats dented on our legs, I asked, "Are you going to confess to what we did, Mo?"

"Why should I?" she said, her wide mouth curling into an impish grin. "Father said we are going to hell anyway, and besides I crossed my fingers so God has already forgiven me, too bad you didn't," she giggled.

She always manages to wiggle out of things, I thought. We hugged and waved goodbye. I ran back to her – "Last touch!"

❧ TAFFY PULL ❧

My father was a man of few words, but when he put his mind to address you verbally, you listened! The hardships he endured as a child growing up in Newfoundland were evident in his masked exterior.

On Saturdays he would try and instill some of this "toughness" on us children. He would line us up like little soldiers, and tell us tales of the hard life, of bread lines and the Depression, and that "Nothing is ever handed to you on a silver plate. You have to work, work, work," he said banging his slide rule on the desk…

One of these days he's going to bust that thing, I thought.

"… and that's the makings of a real man," he continued in a stern voice. Well he forgot about me 'cause I didn't want to be a real man; I was just a little girl, like Shirley Temple. But that was beside the point. In those days children were to be seen and not heard!

What an amusing sight it was – my big brother Johnny standing erect, hoping he wouldn't have to answer any questions – as he wasn't listening anyway! Billy was yawning and wondering, "What if I have to go to the bathroom?" Bobby improvised and stood smartly to attention, pretending he was a soldier being inspected by General MacArthur! Little Dougie was only four. *But give him another four years and he'll be in the front line like us,* I thought, grinning. As for myself, *Sissies,* I thought, *we got a worse grilling from Sister Eulalia, and she didn't care what she hit you with. She was going to make you a soldier of Christ even if it meant rattling your brains with a salt statue of St. Joseph!*

J.W. McCarthy (Jack)   London England
1935

J.W. MCCARTHY

One week, Dad showed us how he invented the first hand skate sharpener ever. It was a neat little steel gadget that slid up and down the blade of your skate and honed it to a sharp edge. He went on in later years to design the first plastic buoy, which helped revolutionize the fishing industry.

What is it going to be this rainy today? I thought, *Please don't let it start with, 'I remember when…'* as I crossed my fingers and held my breath.

After a long silent pause, he settled back in his chair, rested his arms behind his head, stretched his legs lazily and said with a slow smile, "I remember when… as a boy, back in Corner Brook… my father used to make molasses taffy the likes of which you've never tasted." With that announced, he was going to show us how to make good ole Newfoundland molasses taffy!

We stared at each in disbelief. "Did you hear what he said?" I squealed excitedly.

Billy asked, "He's going to what?"

Bobby nudged him in the ribs, cupped his hand to his ear and whispered (like children do), "He's going daffy," he said, "not taffy!"

With that they both howled with laughter, falling over each other. One stern glance from Dad's direction remedied that in a hurry.

He brought out the large cast iron pot, molasses, sugar, soda, vinegar, and then proceeded. He measured carefully. We all huddled around in awe at the transformation that was taking place in our father's character.

Gee, was that a smile I saw there? How handsome he looks! I thought excitedly.

After boiling the syrup, he cooled it in a large pan. He made us wash our hands then grease them with shortening (butter was rationed). He then gave us all a large piece and we all pulled and pulled till it turned a shiny, creamy beige colour.

Bill gave a piece to Bob and he pulled on it so hard he fell to the floor and got taffy all over his britches! Johnny was stuffing it in his mouth as fast as it hardened! Dad then twisted all the taffy in a long satin rope and cut it into bite-sized pieces, letting us eat as much as we wanted! We helped wash up afterward and blew bubbles through a Mason jar ring, all the time laughing and chewing the best-tasting taffy in the whole wide world.

The sun came out filling the room a golden yellow! But somehow I wished it were still raining!

MOLASSES TAFFY

1 cup molasses (Fancy)	¼ tsp cream of tartar
2 cups sugar	2 tbsp butter
1 tbsp vinegar	⅛ tsp baking soda
½ cup water	Pinch of salt

In a medium-sized saucepan, combine molasses, sugar, vinegar and water.

Cook over medium heat until it boils, stirring constantly. Boil covered for 1 minute. Uncover and stir in cream of tartar. Cook until a bit of syrup put in a cold glass of water hardens to a "cracked" stage. Remove from heat, and stir in butter, salt and baking soda. Pour into a buttered plate or pan. Then cool it enough to handle. Grease hands with shortening and pull until it becomes creamy beige colour (about 20 minutes). Twist into long satin ropes and cut into bite-sized pieces with scissors or knife. Enjoy!

∽ MO ∽

Laura Secord, heroine of the War of 1812, was always associated with Québec's *chocolatier.* Every Friday, my little friend Maureen's father, who worked for the Canadian Pacific Railway, used to bring her home six delicious maple walnut chocolates from Laura Secord's sweet shop at Windsor station. Mo would share them with me; only if I allowed her to make fudge at my house, as her strict Aunt Martha wouldn't let her mess up her kitchen.

I pretended that I was Shirley Temple, dining on rich chocolate truffles, and Maureen pretended that she had a mom with a house full of brothers and sisters (her mother died while giving birth to her).

Mo and I had many escapades growing up, nothing very serious, just youthful innocence. She was a high-strung little person, which may have been attributed to her being brought up by a strict Victorian aunt (Martha) who thought picking your nose in public was a sign of severe retardation. When Mo escaped from being slapped, she retaliated by running to our house and hiding under my bed. We would then get up and make a batch of fudge and eat it all up!

After growing into fine young ladies, my family left Montréal. It was a heart-wrenching affair as we tearfully said goodbye, but we did vow to keep in touch.

Years later, I was so excited at meeting my "bestest" friend, as I used to call her. We met at Montréal's Grand Central Station. I strained with anticipation at the thought of seeing my curly topped friend. There she was, hair dyed a "vengeance" blonde and perched proudly on the back of a Harley-Davidson motorcycle with a handsome young man up front. She looked so grown up, but that impish smile was still there! She ran towards me and hugged me fiercely. We laughed and cried at the same time and talked about old times.

"Remember when your aunt invited her Park Avenue friends to your first piano recital, and you pretended to pick your nose behind her back?"

"Remember when we chewed tar thinking it would get our teeth whiter – remember that?"

"Remember when we put rocks in our purses in case boys got fresh and yelled out 'hubba, hubba' but they never did?"

"Remember that crazy letter to 'Dear Miss Dix' and how we wanted to be ... 'In the *know?*'"

"Remember when we pasted your Aunt Martha's falsies on the top of the milk bottle caps, and she almost fainted when the milkman returned them?"

Time was running out, before we knew it was time to say goodbye. "Remember Jen, if you get in trouble, don't forget to cross your fingers," she shouted giggling for she knew I'd run back to her – "Last touch!"

The years blurred by, Mo got married but still lived life on the edge. We went our separate ways but she was never far from my thoughts. In later years, I travelled to Montréal on business. I called her only to hear from her husband the distressing news that my sweet childhood friend had passed away while giving birth under difficult circumstances. It was with great sorrow that I accepted this news; the irony only grew worse as I learned that Mo's husband had found out that her mother had been alive all that time. Her father kept it a secret for all those years and divulged it only on his deathbed. Mo never knew she had a mother, but I took comfort in that I shared my mother with her for a time. Mo gave birth to a beautiful boy called Michael. She also never got to know that I named my baby daughter after her. *Maureen seemed so invincible* I thought, as I walked through the Cemetery on Mount Royal. *We played near here when we were little girls.*

I knelt at her grave and placed a rose where her hands would be. I reminisced to myself and said, "Remember when we kissed the statue of St. Joseph at the Oratory? Well I didn't confess it either, so there!" Through my tears I said goodbye. I could almost hear her mischievous lilting voice saying, "Don't forget to cross your fingers." I smiled as I bent to touch the warm green grass. "Last Touch!"

JEANNETTE AND MO'S VERY SIMPLE FUDGE

This is not a formal recipe

Put enough brown sugar in a saucepan. Add just enough milk (not too much) to melt the sugar. (We used half evaporated milk and half water). Bring to a boil, stirring all the while, (until sugar is melted). Keep boiling. When large bubbles start to form, drop a little of the hot syrup in a glass of cold water. If it forms a hard ball, then it is ready for the next step.

Mo and I used to take turns licking the spoon. Remove from heat and add a blob of butter. Cool for ten minutes. Add a spoon of vanilla, (add walnuts if you like) and beat vigorously until it is no longer shiny (sometimes, it took forever to harden as we hadn't cooked it long enough, if that happens, just boil it again.) Pour into a greased plate, and cut into squares when cool (it never lasted that long).

❧ MADAME JEHANE BENOÎT ❧

In 1979, my sister Linda who was living in Montréal had a boyfriend who was an avid sports car enthusiast. Much to his chagrin, his little MGB sports car was up for sale. An interested caller responded to an ad that he had placed earlier in a Montréal newspaper. He was relocating to New York, where a new job awaited him.

The gentleman caller set up an appointment to view the car the following day. It was a bright sunny morning when they took the long leisurely drive to Québec's Eastern townships. There they came upon a quaint little sheep farm, appropriately named *"Noire Mouton"* (Black Sheep).

"Good afternoon," the gentleman greeted them. "Please come in, *s'il vous plaît!*"

Linda was in awe of this beautiful charming house. *Not a house*, she thought, *a home.*

"Please," he said proudly, "I'd like you to meet my wife, Madame Jehane Benoît."

My sister smiled politely (with all the innocence of a Mary Tyler Moore), as she sat in her kitchen. She had no idea who Jehane Benoît was. She had never learned to cook, and at this point, had no desire to learn!

In her day, Madame Jehane Benoît was Canada's most famous chef. She studied at the Sorbonne and the Cordon Bleu cooking school in Paris, France. In 1973, she was made an Officer of the Order of Canada for her contribution to this art.

The prodigious kitchen looked like an archetype in *Canadian Homes and Gardens*. One could look for an hour and not see the same thing twice, my sister thought. The walls had large built-in racks, filled to capacity with various exclusive wines. Shelves of Mason jars, filled with homemade preserves and rose vinegars, sparkled in the late morning sun.

As Linda sat listening to the soothing, somehow familiar voice of this charming lady, something "clicked" in her mind! "Now, I know who you are," she said excitedly, "you're Madame Benoît. I used to watch you on television right after 'Chez Hélène' when I was a little girl."

Mrs. Benoît was now laughing uncontrollably. She knew all the while that Linda was unaware of her identity.

"How ironic, that I am the one that should be the one to meet you, when my sister Jeannette who owns a French restaurant in Bathurst, New Brunswick, would give her best copper skillet to be in my shoes!" she laughed.

Mrs. Benoît enjoyed my sister's company, and regaled her with stories while the gentlemen were out looking at the car. She told her how she studied food technology in England, her many visits to Paris, and how she fell madly in love with her husband. The thought of him, at this age, having a youthful fling with a little sports car was, in her words *"Magnifique!"*

Linda's boyfriend and Mr. Benoît arrived with grins on their faces, a deal was struck; the shiny green MGB now belonged to the Benoîts. They wouldn't hear of Linda and her boyfriend leaving, without first having lunch, which was served in the bright sunlit dining room.

The lunch consisted of a delectable beef consommé; chilled pheasant salad garnished with geranium leaves; and dropped Yorkshire pudding, with fresh strawberries and clotted Devonshire cream. A robust English tea served in an elegant Royal Doulton teapot made Linda's English boyfriend feel right at home!

They bid their farewells, but not before Madame Benoît signed her current cookbook – Madame Benoit's Lamb Cookbook – and presented it to my sister. It simply said, "To Linda, *la cuisine, c'est l'amour.* Do learn how to do it." Jehane Benoît, Aug/79. And she did!

New Brunswick

∽ THE OLD WHARF ∽

It was 1950 and the little town in New Brunswick seemed so far removed from my beloved Montréal that I reluctantly left behind. *How could my father do this to us?* I thought as I longed for Mo and my other friends. I felt trapped like a butterfly in reverse metamorphosis. *How will I ever get used to not hearing the clanging of streetcars, or seeing Mount Royal, our Jewish and French neighbours, Abe's corner store, and St. Michael's church? Why does life have to be so complicated?*

My father had taken a position as the Mechanical Engineer with Fraser Mills Co. Ltd., which was situated about three miles west of Newcastle. My parents, four brothers, a baby sister and I took up residence in one of the newly built company houses with freshly painted white clapboard siding and black shutters.

They all stood neatly like fancy little dollhouses, and one staff house for dignitaries. Across the street the beautiful Miramichi flowed by.

"I'm almost sixteen and my life is already over," I cried as hot tears fell on my blue poodle skirt. "No one wears saddle shoes out here and all we ever eat is baloney."

Baloney... New Brunswick Steak as it's affectionately called.

"Laissez-faire, ça va passé," my mother smiled.

While it seemed like forever to *passé*, it did however, and I can partly attribute this to Mrs. Murphy the staff house cook. She was a well-fed woman whose culinary skills could tickle the taste buds off any city slicker's tongue that had experienced the pleasure of a "staff house meal." Not everyone escaped her well-honed Irish tongue though.

Mrs. Murphy had a well-rounded face, which often was as sour as Mrs. Wilson's crabapples, and a disposition to match. (Or so she'd have you believe.) At times she softened like the meringue she piled high on the local rhubarb pie and its golden flaky crust.

She knew I had a palate for cooking and let me mess around with her best cast iron pans, but then again I fed her penchant for local town gossip!

"Since yer new to these eer parts, I guess it's me duty to make you aware of the Ghost of the 'Dongarvon Whooper.'" Her voice hushed to a whisper and her eyes narrowed.

"It was a long time ago, in the 1860s, a young Irish camp cook was murdered for his wages, which he had tucked into his shirt, and was slit ear to ear for it. The crew buried him in the deep snow, on the banks of the Dongarvon River. To this very day, if you go deep in the woods you can hear the bloodcurdling eerie screams like the sound of someone gittin' his throat cut... with a dull rusty knife. So beware of frying bacon smells in the woods, as it's jist the ghost of the 'Dongarvon Whooper' and he'll be drawing you in deeper so as to git even with his murderer, he'll gitcha!

"Now don't be going off by yerself into the woods young lady, ye'd look cute now with a slit between yer ears."

Ghost... shmost, I thought. When Mrs. Murphy wasn't spinning yarns and scaring Millie the maid half to death, she'd be flitting about in her kitchen whipping up delicacies from the local harvest. She was a firm believer in using locally grown foods in her vast recipe collection like golden fried fiddleheads; sumptuous baked Miramichi salmon stuffed with wild rice and fresh dill; sweet wild strawberry cobbler; and wild Blueberry Grunt (named from the cooking sounds it makes. (It is Grunt)

Though I missed Montréal dearly, New Brunswick had a quiet naturalness about her that stirred my very soul. I wished Mo could have been with me to share all this.

Our family was just settling into our new home and we hadn't yet adjusted to country living. Because the town's only grocery store (The Beehive) was many miles away, and my parents were negotiating for a car, we had to rely on local entrepreneurs to fill the void.

"Go to the corner store and don't come back wit' any balonee," my mother called out as I headed out the door. The corner store was actually across the long bailey bridge to Derby Junction and was not on a corner, but in Mrs. Flannery's large foyer. It was an old wood framed house tucked in among some lush maple trees near the side of the road. The Flannerys were a friendly lot and never pried in other people's affairs. I'm sure they wondered why we shopped there so often but they never asked.

As I entered the store, the rusty little bell over the screen door tinkled my presence. Mrs. Flannery directed me to the old cooler. There stood rows of Maple Leaf chubs of baloney, standing butt end to attention. I guessed we were not the only ones eating the stuff as I surveyed the abundance of it all. *Gosh, how I'd give my best poodle skirt for just one bite of Ben's Montréal smoked meat sandwich right now,* I thought longingly.

Mrs. Flannery cocked her head in a sympathetic manner and said, "We do have an order of hamburger coming in later on this afternoon."

It was such a glorious day, I thought, *Why not?* "See you later," I said as I skipped out the door towards Wilson's Point.

An old man passed me, "How she going?" he said, not stopping for an answer. I thought I'd reply in the local jargon, "And gidday to you too!" I shouted back.

Following the dirt road around Wilson's Point, I was exploring for a swimming hole when I happened upon a clearing that led me to a path through the woods. In the distance I could see the remnants of an old wharf.

The sun shone beams of misty light through the tall fragrant pines, illuminating a quilt of buttercups and daisies at my feet. Twinkling through the leaves of a silver birch I could see the moving river as the glinting sun merrily danced on top of its multifaceted ripples like a sapphire in a green velvet box.

Birds flitted about from tree to tree, chirping and singing as if welcoming me. I was so caught up in the enchantment of it all, that I climbed the rocks for the first time and dove deep into the cool delicious waters touching the sandy bed that cradled the wondrous Miramichi.

The fast flowing silky water seemed for a moment to lengthen my short dark hair, into long blonde flowing tresses like that of a mermaid, a mermaid who had no use for city shoes.

The land was chaste and unspoiled. The woods were alive with wild berries in the spring and heady with the fragrance of delicate mayflowers. In the distance the compelling trill of the whip-poor-will searching for a mate filled the air. My youthful heart swelled with longing for this perfect place, a place to fall in love!

My brothers and a few friends kept the wharf a secret so its natural beauty would not be disturbed. We erected a diving board from an old plank, which we wedged tightly among the rocks of the abandoned wharf and spent many long and marvelous hours enjoying the simplicity of it.

One hot afternoon as I sat on my favourite log under a tall pine, I heard an unfamiliar huffing sound coming from the trodden path above. It edged closer and closer. My heart was pounding in my ears; I bolted upright, afraid to breathe. I was petrified. I could vaguely make out a portly figure dressed in black, laboring towards me. *Surely it can't be the "Dongarvon Whooper" appearing, sporting a black bowler hat,* I thought. I curiously peered behind him and with relief, saw a chauffeur standing smartly next to a long black car.

"Hot enough for you, young lady?" the intruder asked as he continued on, his sweating face breaking into a massive wide grin. He stood before me and mopped his brow with a white linen hanky. His fine leather shoes were now slowly sinking into the scorching sand. "Sure is hot indeed," he said breathlessly as he stood next to me. "Very hot indeed," he repeated.

Who is this person? I thought and, *what is he doing here anyway?*

"I've always loved it here you know," he continued, "I dream about it in England, and do you know that I used to swim in this very spot when I was a boy?" he said with a faraway look in his eyes. "A lot of good memories, yes indeed, yes indeed."

I offered him a drink of water I had collected from the creek near the bridge. He declined graciously,

"Thank you so much young lady, and what is your name may I ask?"

"Jeannette," I answered.

"Thank you, Jeannette, do enjoy this place as much as I have... enjoy the simplicity of it." And with that he was off. But before he reached the top of the hill, he shouted back, "If you could improve on anything in this area, what would it be?"

That's easy, I thought, "Another diving board!" I shouted back (as my Brother Billy broke the last one while goofing around)

"Done," he answered as he waved goodbye.

Mrs. Wilson, who had noticed the strange car from the road, came running down the path as fast as her legs could carry her. Breathlessly she gasped, "Do you know who that stranger was?"

No, I thought, *but I hope she doesn't tell me it was the Lone Ranger!*

"Lord Beaverbrook, that's who!" (The only Lord I knew was the Lord God.)

"It can't be," I answered, "he introduced himself as Mr. Aitken, Mr. Max Aitken." I said in my best English accent, and with that I dove into the crystal cool water leaving Mrs. Wilson brewing in her pot of Beaverbrook stew!

I returned to explore the old wharf another day and came upon an old gravesite. Pushing aside the decaying leaves, revealed an eroding tombstone, it read: *Mariette, agé 16 ans.* Another grave close by was so ancient that its inscription had worn away with age. *How interesting,* I thought, as I reminisced about my own French background. Could this Mariette be like Longfellow's "Evangeline," and did she run from the English to take refuge in the woods, right here near the old wharf? Did she have a young man who came courting her beneath the tall pines as the summer breezes caressed their faces? And on a moonlit night do their ghostly figures appear as they run through the woods ever so softly so as not to disturb the mayflowers, which are sleeping on the sweet damp earth? I'd like to think so, for whenever I hear the trill of a whip-poor-will, my thoughts gently go back to the old wharf and to unfettered youth.

A goodly time passed, my family moved to Bathurst, New Brunswick. In the meantime, bulldozers leveled our pristine secret place. Shellacked pine picnic tables took precedence over the spread blanket area that we shared for picnics. Gone were the wild blueberry patches to make room for the paved footpaths that lead to the old cemetery. And yes, there stood a tall shiny new modern diving board!

It became the Historical Park and it was another gift he bestowed on the province and he appropriately called it "The Enclosure". It was also deemed a potential site as a mass Acadian burial ground.

As time passed, I had misgivings of that day and thought it best to give due respect to this lord they call Lord Beaverbrook.

There was no shortage of advice as I searched the library on the history of the Aitken family. I was directed to the stately Old Manse Library on Mary Street. There, I met with Dr. Louise Manny, an accommodating lady who was appointed by Beaverbrook to be the first custodian of the gracious old Victorian manse. This was originally the home of Rev. William Aitken, the town's first Presbyterian minister, his wife Jane Noble and their ten children, of which Max (Lord Beaverbrook) was the sixth.

THE OLD WHARF ENCLOSURE

I also learned that he was elevated to the peerage in 1917, and adopted his title from the name of a stream where he fished when he was a boy. Although he was raised in Newcastle, New Brunswick, his business endeavours drew him to England where he entered British politics. He was a very benevolent man and among his many gifts bestowed to New Brunswick was the Beaverbrook Art Gallery in Fredericton.

Dr. Manny preserved a lot of the local history with poetry and songs of yesteryears like "The Jones Boys", "The Ghost of Dongarvon Whooper" and "The Miramichi Fire." The primitive recordings of wailing shanty songs skipped and scratched as they aired on the local CKMR radio station every Sunday afternoon. Mrs. Murphy equated it to a lot of caterwauling.

Beaverbrook was getting along in years and wanted to retire in his beloved New Brunswick but never did. He died in Leatherhead, Surrey, England in 1964. His ashes are housed at the base of a bronze statue situated in the centre of

BEAVERBROOK BUST

the town's square. Many years later I returned to walk the square and stared at the bronze likeness of the man and smiled to myself amusingly and thought, *Diving board indeed!* And I carried on my nostalgic stroll in search of a mermaid, a mermaid I once knew a long time ago…

NORTHWEST BRIDGE FIDDLEHEADS

Fiddleheads are a pan-Canadian delicacy

1 lb fresh fiddlehead ferns

1 cup flour

1 tsp salt

Pepper to taste

3 large eggs

1 tbsp oil

1 tbsp water

1 cup fine dry breadcrumbs

1 cup peanuts (ground)

Peanut oil for frying

Wash fiddleheads in cold water and remove the brown sheaths. Cut off stems. Soak ferns in cold water for 20 minutes.

Mix flour salt and pepper on a plate. Beat together eggs, oil and 1 tablespoon of water. Mix crumbs and peanuts together on a separate plate. Toss the ferns in the flour mixture, then in the egg mixture, and finally, in the peanut mixture.

Let set on sheet until set (about 5 minutes). Deep fry fiddleheads until golden brown. Drain on paper towel.

Serve with drawn butter and fresh lemon.

BLUEBERRY BUCKLE

*So called because the batter, after rising,
sinks to the bottom making the streusel top buckle*

¼ cup butter
½ cup sugar
1 large egg
1 cup all purpose flour
½ tsp salt

1½ tsp baking powder
½ tsp vanilla
⅓ cup milk
3 cups blueberries
1 tbsp lemon juice

TOPPING

1 cup all purpose flour
½ tsp cinnamon

½ cup butter
½ cup brown sugar

Cream butter and sugar; add egg and beat until creamy.

Sift dry ingredients. Add alternately with milk and vanilla. Grease a 9-inch pan and spread batter.

Sprinkle blueberries over batter and drizzle lemon juice over them. Mix dry ingredients with butter by rubbing together with hands until crumbly. Sprinkle over blueberries and bake in a moderate 350°F oven for approximately 30-35 minutes.

This is a favourite dessert in the Maritimes, as its blueberries are the sweetest!

The whole Atlantic seaboard from the St. Lawrence to Cape Breton is quite fascinating. The salted sea breezes release a laissez-faire sensation as you watch the thunderous waves of the mighty Atlantic come crashing on the rocks. It seems to sieve out echoes of the early settlers, when they fished these waters in their tiny boats, many years ago. When you follow the Acadian Trail, you are in union with the past. The continuity of little French villages dot the shoreline, and you may find in amazement, at how little their way of life has really changed, as they cling fiercely to their roots.

When the British captured the French Fort Beauséjour, they took control of the land and rivers as far as Halifax, Nova Scotia. In 1775, they proceeded to evict the French for refusing to pledge allegiance to the English crown. These people are known as Acadians. Some were deported to France and Louisiana where they are now known as "Cajuns."

Families were separated; many were scalped, or starved to death. Countless numbers took refuge in the deep forests and lived there for generations, until they believed their lives were no longer in jeopardy. Their hardships have been recounted through the years and have inspired many poets.

The following is from the epic poem *Evangeline: A Tale of Acadie* (1847) by Henry Wadsworth Longfellow. It is a moving account of the barbaric expulsion of the Acadians in 1775.

Still stands the forest primeval; but under the shade of its branches
Dwells another race, with other customs and language
Only along the shore of the mournful and misty Atlantic
Linger a few Acadian peasants, whose fathers from exile
Wandered back to their native land to die in its bosom.
In the fisherman's cot the wheel and the looms are still busy;
Maidens still wear their Norman caps and their kirtles of homespun,
And by the evening fire repeat Evangeline's story,
While from its rocky caverns the deep-voiced, neighboring ocean
Speaks, and in accents disconsolate answers the wail of the forest.

Today, a forlorn statue of Evangeline sits in a square in Louisiana. The story goes that when Evangeline was torn apart from her betrothed Gabriel on that fateful expulsion day, she was devastated. She searched her entire life for him. In her later years she finds him on his deathbed in Philadelphia where the two share a final kiss as he dies.

The Acadians that did return however settled all over the province. From Restigouche to the north and northeastern tip of New Brunswick in little villages like Shippegen, Lameque, Tracadie, and Miscou. They also went south to Pokemouche and easterly towards Richibucto, Bouctouche, and on to Moncton and Nova Scotia.

Le Pays de La Sagouine (the land of the washerwoman) has a fictitious character created by internationally renowned Acadian author Antonine Maillet from her award-winning book of the same name. The village, which is set on an island in Bouctouche, New Brunswick, is a living village set in natural surroundings. It celebrates Acadian culture by featuring daily live theatre, music, dance and comedy. They speak a colourful language deeply rooted in Acadian culture. If you want to saturate yourself in *Beaucoup de fun,* this is the place to be! (The village is only forty minutes from Moncton.)

Another place to celebrate Acadian culture is at an historic Acadian village that now stands in nearby Caraquet, New Brunswick at the Rivière-du-Nord, which is situated in northeastern New Brunswick. The little village procured authentic buildings from other regions of the province and reassembled them on the site. These buildings are set on former rich marshland worked and drained by the Acadians in the early eighteenth century. Authentically dressed *Acadiennes* in their sunbonnets, these people are direct descendants of a "distinct" society whose very survival was once threatened.

Today, Acadians account for 32 per cent of New Brunswick's population. Louis Robichaud was the first Acadian to be elected premier of the province in 1960. The lifestyle and attitudes of the New Brunswick Acadian far differ from people of other parts of the province. Their music and language are unique to their culture. They speak the same French spoken in their motherland during the seventeenth century. Borrowing words from their English-speaking neighbours, they created a patchwork *patois* that has branched out in various directions through the years. I've heard it good-naturedly referred to as the *"Bi-lingue bi-langue."*

"Joual" is an informal French language that borrows words from the English language. *"Chiac"* is similar and is spoken mostly in the Shediac areas. More than 350,000 Acadians in the Maritimes, Gaspé Peninsula, Îles de la Madeleine, and Newfoundland speak Acadian French. The Brayons or *brayonnes* from Madawaska on the other hand come from the *pays Brayon*, from upper Normandy and are officially recognized as inhabitants of Madawaska. The Brayons cultivated the flax plant, which they processed by shredding and spinning the fibre into clothing. The shredders (pioneers) became known as Brayons. Although they are considered Acadian, their language is closer to that of the Québec dialect.

Many Acadian recipes have been handed down through the generations. Some are curious and some are downright amusing, with a handful of this and thimbleful of that. But the ones that did survive are worth preserving. Acadian cuisine is really an embellishment of wholesome food and I can attest to that; I was brought up on it!

When food was rationed during the war, my mother made *un bon bouillon de poulet (minus poulet) avec des bonnes patates.* With all those *bons* and *bonnes* you almost forgot the absence of a chicken in the pot!

Unlike those who immigrated to Louisiana, the Acadians who remained in New Brunswick spiced their foods with *les herbes salées* (herbs of savory, thyme, and green onion layered in rock salt). The Cajun cuisine of Louisiana on the other hand is a hybrid, a blend of French, Acadian, Spanish, German, Native American, and Afro-Caribbean where most of their sauce piquant originated. But the Acadians brought a cooking style from France with them that embellished otherwise plain or dubious quality meat. Marinades, spices and long cooking in heavy pots produced sauces that stretched the nutritional and filling value to the food. They used whatever was available to them. Fish, potatoes, and

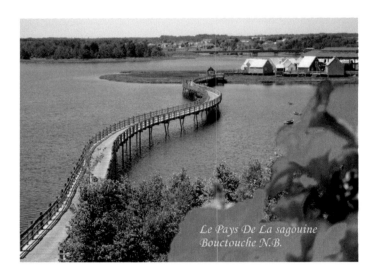

Le Pays De La sagouine
Bouctouche N.B.

salt pork were synonymous with survival in the Atlantic Provinces. When meat was scarce they would shred potatoes, squeeze out the juice in a cloth, roll them into balls and stick bits of fried or sautéed pork into them.

These snow white balls were dropped into boiling water and cooked firm but sticky, and served plain with Ragout gravy, or just plain molasses. These are called *"poutine râpée."* They are not too appetizing looking as they turn a dull grey colour, however, don't let their appearance fool you, as they are delicious! The best ones that I have savored and cannot be compared to any, are "Les Poutines à Leah" in the little town of Bouctouche, New Brunswick. *Poutine Râpée* can be seen on canteen signs (little roadside stands that sell Acadian savories) in the Moncton, Shediac area. It is truly an authentic dish.

POUTINE RÂPÉE

The more flavour in the pork, the better the poutine

There are about as many *poutine râpée* recipes as there are fishing villages that dot the Atlantic seacoast. This is a small recipe, so you can experiment! While recipes vary, two important steps still apply. You must extract as much water from the grated potatoes as possible, and you must keep the water at a boiling point at all times, or else you'll end up with mush!

These poutines are likened to a dirty snowball, but don't let the appearance fool you, as these glutinous potato balls are simply delicious. Many cooks stuff the poutine with tenderized salt pork riblets for even more flavour.

5 medium potatoes (raw)	Salt and pepper
2 medium potatoes (cooked)	¼ Ib salt pork
	Flour for rolling

Have a large pot boiling with 2 quarts of water. Cook 2 potatoes and mash dry over medium heat until smooth. Set aside. Grate 5 potatoes (fine on the grater). Squeeze as much water as possible out of the grated potatoes (wrung out in a clean cloth will do). Dice salt pork, and fry until golden brown and drain on paper towel. Set to one side. Add raw grated potatoes with the mashed potatoes and mix until well blended. Add the salt, and pepper to taste, mix well.

Divide potato mixture into four equal parts. Flatten one part in the palm of your hand; add a small bit of the cooked salt pork in the middle. Form up like a snowball (making sure the pork is well in the middle) and roll into flour. Drop gently into the boiling water. Simmer gently for 1 hour. (It's important to have the water boiling at all times.) Serve with gravy, molasses, or wild berry jam.

CHICKEN BOUILLON (ACADIAN STYLE)

A stewing hen is the secret for a good tasting bouillon.

This recipe makes a large pot enough for a *Reveillon* or family gathering. I find the taste improves overnight. Most Acadian dishes are not stringent when it comes to precise measurements.

5 quarts cold water	2 celery stalks – with leaves
4 lbs stewing hen or other chicken	1 large onion
4 carrots	2 tsp savory leaves
2 tsp salt	1 bay leaf

Chop up stewing hen or chicken. Pour cold water into large pot. Add hen parts and remaining ingredients. Bring to a boil over high heat then reduce heat and simmer for two hours. (Do not add hen meat to bouillon, as the meat is stringy.)

Strain, and cool in refrigerator. When the broth is cold, lift off the layer of fat and use for further recipes. For richer taste add chicken bouillon cubes.

5 lb chicken	4 cups diced potatoes
2 cups carrots	2 tsp thyme
1 cup chopped onions	2 tsp savory
½ cup chopped celery	Salt and pepper

Debone chicken; cut meat in bite size pieces. Heat up hen stock and simmer chicken for 20 minutes. (Simmer bones for two hours, and freeze broth for future use). The longer you simmer the better the broth!

Add remaining ingredients. Cook until vegetables are tender. Ladle into large Bouillon bowls, and serve with hot homemade buns slathered with fresh butter!

ACADIAN BREAD PUDDING

In good conscience, I could not publish this book without inserting the "bread pudding" recipe since homemade bread was eaten at every meal. Whenever I had bread pieces left over, I would throw the bread scraps, raisins and all, into the egg mixture and bake it like that. It was my children's favourite dessert, the brown sauce also helped!

1½ cups milk   ½ cup sugar
½ cup evaporated milk   2 tsp cinnamon
3 eggs (large)   8 slices bread
2 tsp vanilla   ½ cup raisins

In a large mixing bowl, beat eggs lightly. Add all milk, vanilla, sugar, and cinnamon. You may want to trim crusts, however the Acadians left them on.

Butter lightly, and cut in halves. Place in buttered loaf pan. Layer bread and top with raisins. Repeat with remaining bread and raisins.

Pour milk mixture over bread. Press down so all the bread is covered. Leave on counter for 10 minutes.

Bake at 350°F until knife inserted in centre comes out clean, and top is a golden brown. Serve with a brown sauce.

BROWN SAUCE

2 cups brown sugar	2½ tsp cornstarch
2 tbsp butter	1 tsp vanilla
1¾ cups boiling water	

Melt butter. Add sugar. Caramelize over high heat for one minute. Add hot water and stir vigorously until sugar is melted. Stir in cornstarch. Add vanilla, and cook until thickened. Pour over bread pudding.

Fish played a major role in the Acadian's life as it was a primary source of food and is prevalent in many of their recipes. Salmon was a favorite dish served in various ways, including making fish cakes out of it just like they did with their salted cod.

Each year in northern New Brunswick the little town of Campbellton hosts a Salmon Festival where *Ie Saumon est Roi* (the salmon is king!) It even takes precedence over the reigning beauty queen and her court, as its silver foiled gills dazzle in the sunlight in the festival parade. Restigouche salmon is the pièce de resistance on every menu in town. You may have it served any way you like it: smoked, baked, barbequed or fried. If you should ask the locals what they think of Pacific salmon, they'll pause and good-naturedly ask you where you're from first!

ᘯ **MY GRANDMOTHER'S HOUSE** ᘯ

My grandmother's house in the town of Dalhousie was so named after the 9th Earl of Dalhousie in 1837, who was then the governor of Upper and Lower Canada. Dalhousie's first Acadian settlers arrived around 1796; years later in 1820 came a massive wave of immigration. They settled on Chaleur Bay along with the Mi'kmaq First Nation, home to the one of the original peoples of the region. If one stood on the top of the steep "Convent Hill", in the sleepy little town of Dalhousie one could see the sprawling International Paper mill. The IP was the town's most imposing feature. When its smokestack billowed plumes straight up, it offered the locals relief that the cold east wind had finally calmed down. As the sun danced off the waters of Chaleur Bay, one could squint one's eyes and watch a tiny speck grow into a large ship bound for the port of Dalhousie for a load of newsprint.

Around the corner from Convent Hill, a neat white little clapboard house stands proudly on the corner of Duke Street, next to a field of wild flowers. There, sat my grandmother's house. Through my child mind I picture the afternoon sun filtering through the potted red geraniums in my grandmother Roseanne's kitchen windowsill. She was fiercely proud of her Acadian heritage. I always picture her sitting very erect in her rocking chair with the sun shimmering off her white cotton candy hair. The old woodstove's chromed legs reflect off the shiny flowered linoleum floor. A kettle "put on" for a pot of tea is bubbling happily. Navy beans are slowly simmering in a cast iron pot on the back of the stove. They will be then transferred to the oven, with salt pork, molasses, and an onion plopped in the middle. There, they will bake to a reddish mahogany, and produce the best "Down East" pot of beans your mouth has ever had the privilege of eating. Roseanne never followed a recipe, so my mother and I put together this recipe from memory twenty-five years ago. It is as about the closest you can get to the true Roseanne's flavourful beans!

My absolute favourite memory was the delightful warm aroma from a bonne batch of homemade bread cooling on the white painted sideboard. The yeasty aroma fills my nostrils still, as visions of yesteryear floats through the air creating a warm chez nous (homey) feeling. Above my grandfather's rocking chair, a large holy picture of the Blessed Virgin, with a yellowed Palm reverently thumbtacked to her crown, looks down smiling, as if approving all this.

The kitchen was the heart and soul of the home and a gathering place for friends, relatives, and many grandchildren. Roseanne kept everyone entertained; she was a great conteuse (storyteller). She could spin you stories that would render Spielberg breathless. Once she's held you spellbound to her every word, she would embellish her yarn to the pinnacle of suspense. Gappie, (my grandfather) listened and smiled while he contentedly rocked while puffing on his unlit pipe. "In the old days you had to make your own fun," she'd say, as she started tapping a beat with her foot on the floor. "I can remember wearing 'sabots' (wooden shoes, or clogs) and doing this dance," Roseanne would say as she smartly gets up and does a step dance, accompanying herself with her famous tourlout (a form of "Diddle Dum" that was so popular with the early French settlers). There is a definite knack to it, and when mastered it can almost take hold of the dancer's feet! Everyone joins in the contagious woohoo!

Simon plays the fiddle and Gelasse claps time. Uncle Alphonse "clacks" the spoons on his knee, while Archie plays the Jew's harp and Barney clangs a tin pie plate. Meanwhile, Roseanne tourlouts to the tune of St. Anne's Reel, and goes as fast as Don Messer can slide the bow across his fiddle! The old Acadian saying "laissez les bons temps rouler" (let the good times roll) rings true in Roseanne and Gapit's home. They embodied their Acadian culture with faith, love and pride. Sounds fade through time, but embedded memories are the power that interweaves the very soul of one's roots.

ROSEANNE'S BAKED BEANS

2 cups navy beans	1 tsp salt
½ lb salt pork	⅛ tsp pepper
½ cup brown sugar	1 onion sliced
1 tsp dry mustard	1 medium onion (whole)
½ cup molasses	

Wash and soak beans overnight. The next day, place the beans (and same water) in large kettle (add a ½ tsp of soda as it slows gas production) and simmer for up to 1 hour, or until the skins pop open. Cut pork into small cubes and fry until golden brown.

Remove pork cubes. In the hot fat, add brown sugar and caramelize until a deep dark brown. (This gives them that mahogany look!) Strain water from the beans and put aside. Add some of the saved water to the frying mixture (as it facilitates the removal of hard caramel from the pan). Add to this: salt pork cubes, mustard, molasses, salt pepper. In a bean crock or large Dutch oven, add half the beans and put the sliced onions on top. Add the rest of the beans. Pour remainder of liquid and ingredients over the beans. Peel the small onion and prick with a fork and plop it in the centre of the beans. Cook at 250°F for 6 hours. Remove cover during last hour of cooking. Serve with homemade bread!

MOM'S WHITE BREAD

This bread recipe was derived from years of observing my mother baking bread. I loved to watch as she squeaked the bubbles out of the dough for a "Bonne batch de pain!" (Good batch of bread!).

1/2 cup lukewarm water

1/3 cup sugar

2 tsp sugar

2 pkgs. dry yeast (Traditional style)

2 cups milk

2 1/2 cups water

2 tbsp salt

1/4 cup lard or shortening

12-13 cups flour

In the lukewarm water, dissolve the 2 teaspoons of sugar. Sprinkle the yeast over it. Let stand for 10 minutes. Scald the milk in a large saucepan. Add the water, sugar, salt and lard or shortening. Stir until well blended. Cool to lukewarm (this is necessary as any high heat will choke the yeast) then add the east. In a large mixing bowl add the warm mixed yeast mixture. Stir in half the flour and beat with a large spoon. Keep adding flour until you have smooth elastic dough 5-8 minutes. Knead the dough for at least 5 minutes. Turn dough into a large greased bowl, then flip dough over so it greases the top. Cover with a clean cloth and let it raise double in bulk In a warm area. When it has risen once punch down and divide Into 4 balls, or 5 long baguettes. Shape into loaves and let rise until double in bulk about 45 minutes depending on the heat of your kitchen. Bake at 400 degrees for about 30-40 minutes or golden brown. A glaze of beaten whole egg may be brushed on tops for a gold satin finish. For more fine textured bread, let dough rise twice.

∿ LE REVEILLON ∿

It's usually snowing on Christmas Eve in the eastern provinces. Families slowly trudge off to midnight mass as if savoring the magic of this special night. Delicate snowflakes tickle eyelashes, and then gently fall to the sleeping earth.

The church bells are ringing throughout the small towns, calling every one to midnight mass. They sound beckoning, "Come in... come... on" they chime. Candles flicker in frosted windows like so much diamond dust. Carolers singing *"II est né Ie divine enfant"* (the divine child is born) resounds in the crisp night air, and the fragrance of spruce boughs freshens the soul.

Mothers rush home from mass to prepare for the feast. *Le Reveillon* it's called, and it means, "to celebrate all night," and that's exactly what we families do! It's a rather unique French tradition and most French families observe it. In Québec, it's mainly celebrated on New Year's Eve.

The savory smells of homemade meat pies (*tourtières*) filled with pork or beef, topped with a thick golden crust fill the air. There are many versions of meat pies, each cook believes that their recipe is the best, some include potatoes while others believe it's unthinkable to add them... *"Vive la différence!"*

Then there is cipâte or ("C pot", as New Brunswickers call it), which is made with different meats such as rabbit, beef, pork, veal, chicken, and partridge if you're lucky. A special crust is then layered between them, and it is cooked in a slow oven for four hours; it is tender and delectable.

A respectable *Reveillon* would be incomplete without the Chicken Bouillon made with a stewing hen. "The older the hen the better the broth!"

There are baskets of golden-crusted homemade bread, *poutine à la mélasse* (molasses pudding) served with dollops of fresh whipped cream.

Fruit cakes made with suet are proudly displayed.

Menfolk are scooted out of the kitchen as they try to sample the delectable goodies. The house is filled to capacity. Friends and relatives you haven't seen all year greet one another bearing gifts and food. A fiddle appears; singing commences and the *Reveillon* is well under way!

Christmas day and *Reveillon* in Montréal in the 1940s, was a mixture of two cultures: Acadian and Newfoundland.

The Christmas Eve *Reveillon* food was a mixture of Chicken Bouillon, Acadian meat pies, "Jiggs" dinner and Fish'n Brewis. Friends would come calling. My father would pour holiday cheer for the adults and "KIK" cola for us children. We sang Christmas carols. Soon Dad would become all teary eyed as he crooned "Danny Boy" and Bing Crosby's "I'll be Home for Christmas," no doubt reminiscing about the carryings on in his native Newfoundland.

"Right now they'd be having a ball; singing, step dancing and shaking the chimney right up to the rafters," he'd say, with eyes twinkling. We listened wide-eyed no matter how many times he told the story about Christmas "Janneying." How the neighbours and friends would dress up in weird costumes, mostly belted sheets or blankets with slits for eyes, how they spoke in low guttural sounds, disguising their voices and once identified, were told to "uncover," then treated to sweet cakes and a wee bit of the "hard stuff". (The "Janneying" tradition parallels the Acadian custom, the only difference is that they celebrated it one day in Lent and it's called "*Mi-Carême*").

As the evening wore on, my father basked in the glow of the festive "spirit," as he recounts his friends, the Cantwells, Pitmans, and the gentle snow falling on the beautiful Humber River. His Irish accent thickens as he thinks sadly of his friend "Joey" (Premier of Newfoundland) and the pending Confederation, a move not so well received by many Newfoundlanders abroad. At about this time of evening, my mother sensing the mood had the courage to interject and tell stories and funny anecdotes about her Acadian traditions. As always, my uncle Gordon would pipe up and say, "Come on girl, give us a song." My mother would stand up tall and lead them into a French song that somehow everyone knew. "*Alouette... gentille alouette.*" And guide them through each body part. We children chuckled as the Newfoundlanders twisted their tongues around "*Je te plumerais*" and "*et la tête*"... "*Alouette.*"

It was all in good fun.

Because Christmas dinner was served at lunchtime, (an early maritime tradition) the tantalizing smells of turkey and savory stuffing wafted through the house during mid-morning, intensifying the holiday spirit.

Over the large well-worn kitchen table, a freshly ironed white linen tablecloth that my mother had brought with her from home, draped over the sides touching our laps.

A golden-crusted turkey served on a milk china platter was decorated with bouquets of savory and thyme. Red wax candles and fresh sprigs of spruce boughs served as a centrepiece. The pretty mismatched flower china settings held bright red and green "cracker" pulls with favours and paper hats inside. The sideboard held steaming bowls of creamy mashed potatoes, fragrant dressing, spiced root vegetables, crusty homemade bread and gravy. For dessert there was spiced cake, "Poutine a trou", an Acadian apple dessert, and Newfoundland's "Figgy Duff", which is a molasses pudding. Mom made gingerbread men out of her molasses cookie recipe; I helped make smiley faces with raisins on them.

I live in Vancouver now, and still celebrate *Reveillon*. But when I smell the savory fragrance of Christmas, my heart quickens back to a simpler gentler time of life called "reverence."

MOM'S MOLASSES COOKIES

This recipe has been in our family for generations.

It makes a good batch of soft tasty cookies. This recipe calls for plain molasses, which is today's "Fancy" molasses. For a less sweet and darker cookie, use "cooking molasses".

1 cup shortening (I use butter)	2 tsp baking soda
1 cup sugar	4¾ cups all-purpose flour
1 cup molasses "fancy"	1 heaping tsp each of cinnamon,
2 large eggs	cloves, ginger, allspice
½ cup hot water	¼ tsp salt

In a large bowl, cream shortening and sugar until smooth. Add eggs and molasses and beat well. Add baking soda to the hot water. Mix spices and salt into the flour, and add to the molasses mixture alternating with the hot water and soda. Batter will be quite thick. Chill for one hour.

Roll (lightly) out on floured board at about. Cut in desired shapes.

Cook at 375°F for 12 minutes or until crisp around the edges.

ACADIAN TOURTIÈRE

There are many variations of meat pies "Down East."
This is my version.

1 double crust favourite	¼ cup celery leaves (chopped)
pastry recipe	1½ tsp savory
1 lb lean pork (diced)	1 tsp thyme
1½ lbs beef (diced)	1½ tsp salt
3 med. sized onions (chopped)	⅛ tsp pepper
1 cup potatoes (diced)	Flour

Place all the meat in a frying pan along with 2 of the chopped onions, and cook until lightly browned. Transfer meat into a saucepan, and pour enough water to barely cover. Cover and simmer for 1½ hours.

When meat has tenderized, add the remaining onion, plus potatoes, celery, sage, savory, thyme, salt, and pepper to taste. Simmer for 20 minutes. Add flour to remaining juices, to make very light gravy.

Cool, and pour into pastry-lined dish and cover with a top crust.

Bake at 375°F until golden brown.

FIGGY DUFF

2¼ cups stale breadcrumbs
1-cup sultana raisins
¾ cup table molasses
¼ cup soft butter
½ tsp ginger
⅛ tsp cloves
1 tsp allspice

1 tbsp cinnamon
⅛ tsp nutmeg
¼ tsp salt
1 tsp baking soda
1 tbsp hot water
½ cup sifted unbleached flour

Soak bread in water for 5 minutes. Squeeze out water. Combine crumbs, raisins, molasses soft butter, spices and salt. Add the soda which been dissolved in the hot water. Mix thoroughly. Add the sifted flour. Mix well. Spoon into a pudding bag or greased mold and secure tightly. Cover and simmer on low heat for 1½ - 2 hours.

This pudding is similar to the traditional English "Bag pudding".

Newfoundland

After the expulsion, when their fortress fell in 1758, the Acadians from the Minas Basin of Nova Scotia fled to Newfoundland. There, they took refuge in the coves of Bay St. George and the Port-au-Prince peninsula, where they settled. The interweaving of the British and Acadian cultures along with the Scottish, Irish, Channel Islanders, and Mi'kmaq's enriched Newfoundland's history.

Fishing and Newfoundland are synonymous. It was always the dominant industry, but the economy collapsed in the Great Depression of the 1930s and the people voluntarily relinquished their independence to become a British colony again. Prosperity and self-confidence returned during and after the Second World War. With the support of Joseph R. Smallwood, then Premier of Newfoundland, the colony joined Canada as its 10th province on March 31, 1949 after two years of intense debate and referendum.

Squid Jiggin' Ground
—Arthur Scammell (1928)

"This is the place where the fishermen gather in oilskins and boots and Cape Anns battened down; all sizes of figures with squid lines and jiggers, all congregate here on the squid jigging ground."

"O, we'll rant and we'll roar like true Newfoundlanders; we'll rant and we'll roar on deck and below; until we touch bottom inside the two sunkers; and straight through the channel to Toslow we'll go."

Toslow was named by the French settlers. It means *tasse d'argent* (silver cup for the shape of its harbour).

Cod was a mainstay of many a diet and a traditional dish for the locals. Whenever a Newfoundlander thinks of fish he naturally thinks of cod. Other fish are referred to by name (so if you're yearnin' for a bit o' Halibut, you'd better make it clear!). Housewives devised ingenious and delicious recipes containing the cod that are revered to this very day.

Most Newfoundlanders love salt cod. They utilized every part of the fish, even its tongue! Cod-tongues are tender and succulent and even found their way on many menus in gourmet restaurants all across Canada.

Fish cakes made with salt cod are not only popular with Newfoundlanders, but on meatless Fridays they found their way to many a New Brunswicker's family table.

One traditional dish that is quite familiar to most people is the beloved "Fish 'n Brewis." This is boiled salt cod and "hard tack" (a dry sailor's biscuit) that is softened in water, then boiled and served with "scrunchions" or "cracklings" (cubed salt pork fried to a crispy golden brown). Newfoundlanders use and consume all fruits of the sea, even seal.

Seal flipper pie is a gourmet's delight. If you are fortunate enough to find a seal that is not sweetly smiling back at you on the cover of any wildlife magazine, then you're in luck.

Newfoundlanders would smack their lips with delight at the thought of luscious seal flipper pie, crowned with a thick golden crust, and cooked to perfection in an old woodstove.

Capelin – food fit for the gods – my father would say through squinted eyes as he cogitated images of these rich and succulent morsels from his homeland. The very word would set an ordinary "New Foundlander" ranting and roaring with delight! Those smoked silvery little fish he saw in his mind's eye were as he tasted them, corned, fried, baked and dried, (all doing an Irish jig inside his head!) He would say, "There's nothing better than a heaping plate of smoked capelin washed down with Demerara rum" (sailor's milk he called it). The most familiar known Atlantic rum is called Newfoundland "Screech". The first screech was brought from British Guyana by a fishing crew. Since it was very heavy potent rum, the locals diluted it and sold it for fifty cents a bottle. Screech was very popular with the Royal Canadian Navy.

How did it get its unusual name? An army officer was reprimanding a young soldier on his bizarre behaviour and asked for an explanation. He answered, "It's the drink, sir, I take a drink ... walk a block, run a block ... then 'screech' a block!"

Enjoy the recipes given here. If you haven't tasted Newfoundland cuisine, you will be in for a treat. "God willing, may you always have Hashin's on your plate!" (May you never run out of food.)

JIGGS DINNER

This is a boiled dinner that consists of beef brisket with cabbage, turnips, carrots and potatoes. A gauze bag filled with yellow peas is thrown into the pot and then cooked tenderly, absorbing the delicious flavours. When cooked, the "pudding" is removed from the pot then sprinkled with salt and pepper then mashed into a golden amber. Large dollops of country butter melt lazily into rivulets of steaming hot Pease pudding, which is the perfect accompaniment for this simple dish.

JIGGS DINNER

This traditional dish will fill at least 6-8 hungry stomachs on a bitter winter's day!

¾ lb salt meat (ribs or corned beef)   1 large cabbage head
2 cups yellow split peas   2 large onions
8 potatoes (peeled)   1 large turnip (peeled)
6 carrots (peeled)

Soak salt meat overnight in cold water (do not soak the corned beef). Soak yellow peas (with a pinch of soda) in cold water overnight. Next day, drain and add fresh water. Bring meat to a slow boil. Boil for 1 hour.

Meanwhile drain the soaked peas. Wrap in cheesecloth (allowing space for expansion) and tie with a string. Put in boiling pot with meat and slow boil for 1 hour or until the meat is tender.

Meanwhile prepare vegetables. Quarter the potatoes, cut carrots and turnips in large pieces. Cut onions in half, and cabbages in wedges. Add the turnip and carrots to the pot. Cook for 20 minutes, then add potatoes, cabbage and onions. Cook 20 minutes (or until tender).

Remove "Pease" pudding 10 minutes before serving. Remove cheesecloth. Correct seasoning. Add large dollop of butter and mash to a creamy consistency. Serve with the meat and vegetables.

This, my dears, will tickle the taste buds of any Mainlander that used to call "The Rock" home!

FISH 'N BREWIS

This is an overnight recipe

2 lbs salt cod   ½ lb salt pork"
4 cakes "Hard tack" bread   1 med. onion

"Hard tack" is called a "sea biscuit" because when kept dry it can last for years. The word Brewis is derived from the word "bruise", meaning to break up and bruise the hard bread into pieces. Purity Company has been producing hard tack for

Newfoundland since 1924. I always keep some on hand for my Christmas buffet. This simple dish has a unique taste and texture.

Split four hard tack bread or biscuits. Cover with water and soak overnight.

Rinse and skin the salt cod and cut soak overnight in cold water. Next day drain fish and rinse well. Cover with cold water and slowly simmer until tender.

Meanwhile, use the same water and boil biscuits for 2 minutes. Drain immediately. Keep hot.

Cut salt pork into small pieces and fry to a golden brown called "Scrunchions". Save pork drippings.

Chop onion into small pieces and fry in the pork drippings. Flake salt cod and mix with cut up hard bread and onions. Drizzle pork drippings over entire dish and garnish with Scrunchions. Salt and pepper to taste.

⤮ BAKEAPPLE PIE ⤮

Bakeapple, referred to by Newfoundlanders, is a unique berry found growing on low plants all over the island. This plump yellow berry with the characteristics of a raspberry, has nothing to do whatsoever with apples, despite what the name implies! The name was so derived when the French settlers asked the English settlers *"Bai qu'appelle?"* (which in French, means, "What is the name of this berry?") So, in all the confusion, the compromised name Bakeapple stuck to this very day. It makes delicious jams and jellies and you may see it so named on gourmet shelves everywhere.

BAKEAPPLE PIE

⤮

3 cups bakeapples or cloudberries	¼ tsp nutmeg
¾ cup sugar	1 tbsp butter
¼ cup flour	1 favourite double crust pastry recipe

Mix the bakeapple with sugar, flour, and nutmeg.

Line the bottom of a pie plate with pastry. Fill pie shell with bakeapple mixture. Dot the pie with pieces of butter. Cover with pastry and slit to allow for steam escape. Brush with egg white wash.

Bake at 400°F for 15 minutes. Reduce heat to 350°F and bake for approximately 35 minutes.

Bake on bottom rack of oven until pie is a golden brown.

New Brunswick

✦ A SHORT HISTORY ✦

What New Brunswick lacks in affluence compared to the other more prosperous provinces in Canada, it makes up for in natural beauty.

New Brunswick is the only province deemed truly bilingual. The French and English have lived side by side for hundreds of years. Among the antecedent people were the Mi'Kmaq natives who were originally from the "People of Dawn" but withdrew when other tribes made treaties with the white man. The Mi'kmaqs, it was thought, never signed treaties.

DID YOU KNOW THAT...

🍁 New Brunswick is the home of the famous Atlantic lobster, the Miramachi salmon, and the fiddlehead? The delicious delicate ostrich fern that announces spring in the Maritimes was so revered, that in 1945, they named Canada's oldest literary journal *The Fiddlehead*, which is published by the University of New Brunswick.

* The world's first chocolate candy bar originated in St. Stephen, New Brunswick. It first appeared in 1906, an invention of the Ganong family and soon copied the world over.

* Benedict Arnold was a resident of New Brunswick. He was among the American refugees who settled in St. John, New Brunswick in 1776. He was so unpopular with the Loyalists that he left with his family in 1791 for Britain.

* New Brunswick was also home to famous Canadian painters such as Alex Coleville, Lawren Harris, Miller Brittain and Jack Humphrey.

* The world's largest covered bridge, which spans 1,282 feet over the St. John River, is situated in Hartland, New Brunswick and opened in 1901.

* Another largely unrecognized New Brunswick invention was Canada's first automobile. It was a three-wheeled "horseless carriage" built by Thomas Turnbull in St. John in 1851, propelled at thirty miles per hour and made of wood.

* In the late 1800s at Janeville, New Brunswick, a law was passed prohibiting children being fed lobster sandwiches, (considered the poor man's lunch) more than twice a week.

Where else in Canada could one find such colourful and compelling names of counties, towns, rivers and parks such as … Kouchibouquac, Tabisintac, Mactaquac, Buctouche, Richibucto, Memramcook, Nashwaak, Esquiminac and Pokemouche. Bathurst, New Brunswick is a city by the harbour on the beautiful Chaleur Bay – French in flavour, yet bilingual in practice. This is where our family lived, where free enterprise is alive and well. It is home of the "Hospitality Days" Festival and beautiful sandy beaches at Youghall, Caron Point, and Chaleur. Three enchanting waterfalls – the Tetagouche, Grand, and Papineau – are in the nearby vicinity.

Bathurst is home of the famous "Danny Burger", the Atlantic host and Danny's Motel, a tribute to Danny DeGrace and his wife Adeline who started it all with a small diner in Beresford in 1947.

Bathurst is where Frank Mersereau, former owner and editor of *The Northern Light* newspaper, encouraged me to write this book over twenty-five years ago. He submitted and published my many tongue-in-cheek anecdotes on child rearing to the *Star Weekly* in Toronto in the late sixties.

Bathurst was home to my family and parents for a number of years, where we developed many friends through the church, mining industry and curling club.

THE GLOUCESTER HOTEL
BATHURST, NEW BRUNSWICK

∾ LA CORBEILLE ∾

The only element deficient in the City of Bathurst was its noted lack of fine dining restaurants. That's when I made the conscious decision to turn in my real estate licence for a fine copper skillet and open a French restaurant, in the old Gloucester Hotel on the corner of Douglas and Maine. This fine structure was at one time the region's most elegant and prestigious hotel. It was purchased in about 1922 by John P. Leger, an entrepreneur who first introduced electricity to Bathurst. His son, Arthur Leger, had a sports fishing lodge nearby and supplied the elegant dining room with fresh seafood year round.

The establishment was quite precocious for its time, considering its pristine location, nestled in a little town near Chaleur Bay. K. C Irving and M. J. Boylen were among the many distinguished guests who frequented the hotel. In later years it was purchased by Harper Kent who continued to a degree to offer New Brunswick's finest dining on the North Shore.

La Corbeille was opened in 1979 with Mayor John Duffy officiating. Seafood played a large part in our daily food preparations, as it was the mainstay of the menu. Lobster, salmon, cod, haddock, sole, and especially Nova Scotia's Digby scallops were among the many fish that were harvested daily and ended up in La Corbeille's cast iron kettles. Local herbs and vegetables complemented the many dishes. Butter was churned most mornings to complement the freshly baked crusty rolls and French bread.

Our clientele included professionals from various local business establishments. However, our most prolific clientele were from the mining community such as Brunswick Mining and Smelting and Noranda Mines. One manager was such an avid regular that he insisted I cook his steaks in his own copper pan, where it mindfully hung in my kitchen.

I have fond memories of one occasion, when Mr. Young, the general manager of East Coast Smelting (Noranda Division) in Belledune, was to entertain mining executives from Europe. There was to be a party of approximately thirty people. When I discussed the menu with Mr. Young (who was so proud of La Corbeille), he just smiled and said, "Give them a lobster feast they'll never forget!" We closed the dining room to the public, and awaited their arrival. The buffet table was decorated with an authentic lobster trap (from a local fisherman) filled with New Brunswick wildflowers. Unbeknownst to me, Mr. Young, decided to prank his guests. He directed his driver to the back of the hotel's entrance, which typically was overflowing with garbage bins up to the rickety steps. Meanwhile, in the dining room, dressed elegantly in my tailored cream jacket and long skirt, my eyes quickly darted to the swinging kitchen doors and my nervous kitchen staff. I stood slack-jawed at the sight, but soon gave in to the boisterous laughter that ensued. "Not to worry

Janet, (as I was known as then) I had to show them what a diamond in the rough your beautiful restaurant is", he said with an impish grin.

The menu for the evening was Lobster Bouillabaisse, Lobster Thermidor, and freshly caught lobsters boiled in local seawater. China platters proudly displayed mounds of warm cracked lobster. There were baskets steaming with hot French baguette, large individual silver bowls of drawn butter for dipping and various piquant sauces to tickle the palate!

Nestled among the silver tureens, and brimming with steaming lobster bisque were red lobster claws buoyed on top of swirled *crème fraîche*. To tease the senses, Coquille St. Jacques shells, filled with velvety wine sauce and plump Digby scallops, fluted with whipped Prince Edward Island potatoes, waited on starched doilies to delight the palate of the guests with this elegant appetizer. A gentleman from France, in the midst of lip smacking and utterances of *"incroyable!"* and *"c'est fomidable!"* (music to a chef's ears) raised his glass and proposed his comrades join him in a toast to Bathurst and one of the finest restaurants that he'd ever had the pleasure of dining in. I knew then that I had arrived. Well, all except for the back entrance caper!

LOBSTER BISQUE À LA CORBEILLE

2 lobsters	4 tbsp butter
2 tbsp butter	½ cup flour
1 onion (minced)	1 quart fish or chicken broth
1 tsp tarragon leaves	(boiled)
2 tbsp celery leaves	½ cup cream
½ cup white dry wine	1 tbsp butter
1 cup broth (fish or chicken)	Sprigs of fresh tarragon

Crack lobster claws, tail, and body parts (removing sack and spongy tissue). Add the pieces of lobster (shell and all) in frying pan and sauté in 2 tablespoons of butter with onions, tarragon and celery, for about 5 minutes or when the meat turns red. Add wine and broth. Cover and simmer for about 20 minutes.

Remove meat from the pan and take out as much lobster from the shells as possible and chop it finely. Set to one side. Save the shells and reserve the liquid.

In a saucepan mix 4 tablespoons of butter and cook the roux until thickened and light brown. Add the boiling broth and whisk over medium heat until thickened. Chop remaining parts of lobster, discarding the head. Add shells to the saucepan with the lobster meat, tarragon, celery, salt, wine, and broth.

Simmer for 2 hours. Strain through a fine sieve, (or cheesecloth) bring to a boil and add cream, correct seasonings. Float sprigs of fresh tarragon on top of each serving.

Serve with a warm baguette of French crusty bread!

ꙮ THE GLOUCESTER DINING ROOM (EARLY 1960S) ꙮ

The Gloucester's kitchen (the heart of the hotel) was the domain for some very fine and colourful cooks, like Herb Robertson whose temperament was as fickle as the east wind that blew across the Bathurst Harbour. Herb, who hailed from Tabisintac, gained a bit of local notoriety for his Parker House rolls, succulent clam chowder, and throwing an occasional pot across the kitchen counter! Despite his idiosyncrasies everyone loved him. Another well-known cook was Dora, who managed the Carleton Grill and delighted everyone with her wonderful decadent "Mile High" pies. Many still remember Dora from the good old days. She always good naturedly reminded the local Catholics when it was Friday, and that you had to order fish instead of the "hot hamburger" with a mountain of French fries, gravy, and peas that your mouth was drooling for!

FLYING MRS. CHATELAINE

Two events of my life in New Brunswick in the 1970s have gained me some recognition and notoriety throughout the Maritimes.

First, my only sister, Linda, who was teaching at O'Sullivan College (private school for young ladies) in Montréal had been monitoring my activities during her younger years and thought of me as an inspiration to all women (as most younger sisters do). She wanted me to submit my thoughts, writings, and accomplishments for her "provocation" class. I was more than flattered and complied by submitting with a larger than needed manuscript.

After utilizing its contents, (and unbeknownst to me) she then popped it into an envelope and shipped it off to Chatelaine, one of Canada's leading women's magazines, entering the Mrs. Chatelaine Contest.

A considerable time had passed, when one day I received a surprising, thought-provoking phone call. The lady caller was congratulating me on representing New Brunswick in the Mrs. Chatelaine Contest, and that I was the proud recipient of a gold watch and a blender!

Bathurst Hospitality Days organizers invited me to appear in the Hospitality Days Parade, which I accepted hesitantly. Perched on the back of a red convertible with two of my daughters, and a "Mrs. Chatelaine" banner flapping in the breeze, we took our place in line behind Premier Richard Hatfield's convertible. The premier smiled back at us and then turned to his aide and asked, "What's a Mrs. Chatelaine?" (He's long since graced their pages).

Whenever I hear K.D. Lang's soulful rendition of "Miss Chatelaine", I smile amusingly to myself and reflect on the hilarity of it all.

Secondly, flying was my coolest undertaking on the threshold of turning forty. I remember my first solo vividly. The aircraft were fixed wing Cherokees. After many hours of training, I was ready for my maiden flight.

Finally… throttle in slowly… with the engine roaring deafeningly down the runway, the grass a blurred ribbon of green, the aircraft lifted skyward. I was flying!

Quivering with excitement and soaring emancipation, I physically embodied the thrill of the moment as I was flying under my own resources. With the thump of my heartbeat competing with the roar of the engine, I banked the aircraft to the left and surveyed the earth below. The jagged shoreline of Chaleur Bay dotted with the white buoys of salmon nets, looked inversely reposed in tranquility. As my throttle grip slackened, I pleasured in the sun's rays, as they playfully danced on seagull's wing. In my mind's eye, I was among them.

I surveyed the windsock indicating the east wind was dangerously strong. "Tower to XAY Chickadee… return to runway one niner… over," the radio crackled. My virgin flight was over. Reluctantly I returned to base and my only perfect three-point landing! As I walked to the tower base, my feet never touched the ground, my head was in the clouds, even the bucket of ice water that the other pilots threw on me as an initiation ritual, didn't faze me. While the other pilots clipped their ties, which adorned the walls in honour of their first solo, I retreated to the ladies room where I removed my bra and hung it proudly amongst my male counterparts – strange bedfellows indeed!

Janet Hartle sits at her Cheroke Piper after just completing her first solo flight at the Bathurst airport after flying off and on for thee months.

The Northern Light 1974

JANET HARTLE (AS JEANNETTE USED TO BE KNOWN AS)

ᎦᎷ **MAGIC MITTENS** ᎦᎷ

It was in the early 1970s and the little city of Bathurst, New Brunswick was covered in a thin layer of white powdery snow. The frigid wind scoops little puffs of snow in the air where it settled into crevices of the windowpanes, created a frosted effect.

Lady, our German Shepherd, lay quite content on the warm floor next to the pile of rock samples. She nuzzled close to my father's foot, sniffing his damp woolen socks as he wearily removed them... another exhausting day of staking near his Silver Jack Mine.

My father had left the engineering field for quite a few years now, and had pursued geology as it applied to the mining and mineral exploration industry. He occupied the basement suite of our home for a time and made it into a nest of sorts, surrounded by rock samples, books, magnifying glasses, tons of paper and an old Underwood typewriter. On the carriage of the typewriter was a half written letter to the N.B.P.D.A. (New Brunswick Prospectors and Developers Association) of which he was president. It read in part, "That the campaign will be continued against barricades, fences, bulldozed blockades and gates at the entrances of roads leading to Crown lands, the virgin prospecting territory of our country." Dad was a maverick, and a fighter, and lord help those who stood between him and a claim post! They didn't call him "Silver Jack" for nothing. He lifted his dusty old packsack weighted with rocks. He moved his prospector's pick to one side and dug deep into its far-reaching confines, and emerged with a bottle of Bacardi.

Just enough for two good drinks, he thought, as he carefully poured a hefty shot into two mugs. He then filled them with steaming hot water, added a bit of honey and floated a nugget of butter on top.

Three knocks of the broom handle on his kitchen ceiling ensured my hasty descent. "You all right?" I asked as I poked my head in the door.

"Come in, take a load off your feet girl, and have a hot toddy, it's going to be one hell of a cold winter," he said in his imposing voice, "and besides I want you to taste my rabbit stew."

As I sat at his table I thought, *Who could resist a taste of his tantalizing rabbit stew, with its delicate dumplings?* One thing for certain, old Jack was a remarkable cook. "See that box over there?" he asked grabbing it and dumping its contents all over the floor. A dozen multicoloured mittens lay scattered haphazardly on the rug. "There's not one damn good pair in the lot." They looked perfectly good to me.

"I'll be going to Labrador soon for a bit of prospecting and I'll be needing some decent mitts to take along with me. Why no one can make mitts like the fishermen's wives used to make when we were a British colony back then, is beyond me!" he said all in one breath.

What it all came down to was this: as a young boy growing up on the coast of Newfoundland, he recalled the men of his village wearing mitts of a quality he has not seen since — as if blaming Confederation for their extinction.

These wondrous mitts, when used for hauling in the nets or jigging cod, never got soaked, and kept the most calloused hand as warm as a toasted Capelin. *What were these magic mitts made out of?* I wondered.

"Wool girl, wool," he said, as if reading my very thoughts.

He had snippets of early recollections like — some relative shearing a sheep and helping his mother card the wool. He searched in vain for years for the perfect mitt. The start of every winter would invoke his ongoing quest. At one point he had two Mi'Kmaq Indian ladies knitting up a storm in hopes that their ancestral lineage could somehow conjure up the mittens that he so dearly craved.

When explaining the pursuit to his friends, they'd say. "Give it up, old Jack" and assured him that it was just wishful thinking on his part. He seemed defeated, as he thought of how he left all this behind when he sailed from Port aux Basques, Newfoundland bound for Canada... a long time ago. It was not just a mitten he was after, I thought, it was also a piece of the past.

Well, this fascinated me as I contemplated it. *If the memory endured for so many years, then it must be so.*

"There must be a way!" I announced jumping away from the table, inadvertently knocking my hot toddy to the floor and onto the strewn mittens. *You'll not be needing these anymore as I'm going to make you the mittens you've been searching for, or die trying,* I thought as I threw a mitten to the ceiling.

First, I needed wool. My thoughts immediately turned to my friends the Wisemans, who owned a sheep farm on the outskirts of town. It sounded so noble, and little did I know what was in store for me!

They shared in my enthusiasm as I tried to fill them in on this exciting quest I was on. Jim Wiseman just shook his head and smiled, but could not comprehend the desired results (neither could I at this point) but gave me enough wool, (a whole sheep's worth) and a pair of carders.

As I entered the kitchen, the stench of unwashed raw wool wafted behind me. My father charged by me with all the grace of a bull moose plowing through a bramble thicket, stopped dead in his tracks, and gave me a "What's-that-awful-smell" look, which made me laugh out loud, as the reek of smoked capelin fish crisping on his bare stovetop could beat this smell any day!

After many washings of the wool, there it lay as soft as any cloud that floated over the Humber River! The next step was carding. Dad took to it as if he'd been doing it for a living, but he didn't think I noticed the lump in his throat as he held the wool cards in his hands while he combed the wool into fine rolls. It was as if the years rolled back one by one softening his face like that of a child, but upon sensing my presence, he'd correct his posture and resume his normal stern determined look that we all knew so well.

For days I washed, and he carded; with magic mittens firmly planted in our minds, we continued both day and night. The next step was deciding the size of these mitts, as I had to allow for a lot of shrinkage. The downfall of every mitt was that, "The darn things were never big enough!" he'd say, and besides they had to be large enough to fit over his parka sleeves.

Well, by golly this mitt is going to be large enough, I thought as I cut out the following measurements on some newspaper: twenty-four inches long, by twelve inches wide! I must say that I looked at it with some reservation and wondered laughingly if I hadn't exaggerated my measurements a little. But, upon seeing them, dad became ecstatic. "That's it!" he roared, "That's it."

This boosted my spirits, and off I was on my magic mitten cloud once more. But spinning proved to be a stumbling block. No matter how loose, or tightly we spun, it never was quite right. Dad was not saying too much, and looked a little discouraged. "We can't give up now can we?" he asked pleadingly.

"Give up after all this? *Never!* I'll finish these mitts even if I have to glue them together!" I answered graphically.

As I sat among the rolls of carded wool I thought, *There must be a better way... why not knit up the rolls just as they were without spinning them. It would be like knitting right off the sheep's back.* I laughed to myself. Easier said than done! The first few rows were torturous. Casting the three-inch rolls into stitches became a laborious task. Large blisters quickly formed on my two index fingers making the work even more painful.

Only two more rows, I thought, *and see if it can be done...* knit one, pearl one. Dad was pretentiously coming in from time to time, but all in the aid of casting a watchful eye at success or failure.

Slow and steadily, I plodded along as I knitted four inches of ribbing. *By George, I think I've got it!* I was really getting the knack of it, and was actually proud of my blisters!

After a week of knit one pearl one, there emerged a soft downy white gauntlet that "The Friendly Giant" could wear as a boot! I secretly hoped no one caught a glimpse of it before I had a chance to shrink it to a decent size!

After a few days of hot water washings it had "felted" beautifully. It was still quite large I thought, but remembered, the downfall of every mitt was that it was never large enough! I also plunged it into cold water and it hadn't soaked through! He was right, the resin in the raw wool acted as a waterproofing agent.

As I sat alone at the kitchen table I gazed at the fluffy white mitten. He stood up slowly, a look of disbelief and awe crossed his ace. "My gawd, you've really done it!" he said softly, his eyes brimming.

Now I know why he was so obsessed with the wanting. I thought of both the physical and mental aspects of

creating this "small piece of the past." The wool created the warmth; the felting provided insulation; the resin and lanolin provided waterproofing; the carding the train of thought; and the knitting the strength, love, and lesson!

With a sigh, I gently cradled the finished mitt in my arms, and hugged it tightly, as if trying to squeeze all my love into the tiny rows of wool my father carded... somehow I wished it could hug me back. Wiping my tears, I walked slowly into my father's room. He was sitting among the rolls of wool carding, with visions of magic mitts, his mother, and a little fishing village in Newfoundland.

"So, Silver Jack, is this the mitt you lost a long time ago?" I asked as I proudly held the gauntlet high! Brimming with tears, he shoved his hand deep into the mitt like it belonged there.

"*Unbelievable!*" he said. "A real man's mitt, a mitt from home, I'd say it's a *Magic Mitten*." He smiled, shook his head and went back to carding.

SILVER JACK'S RABBIT STEW

1– 2 lb rabbit
¼ lb salt pork
½ cup flour
1 clove garlic
1 tsp savory
2 med. onions (chopped)

2 cups chicken broth
2 carrots (chopped)
2 large potatoes (quartered)
6 large spinach leaves
Salt and pepper

Cut rabbit in quarters. Cut salt pork in cubes and fry until crisp (crackling). Remove crisps and set aside.

Dredge rabbit pieces in flour and salt and pepper. Fry rabbit in reserved fat until golden brown. Remove and set aside. In same pan fry chopped onion and garlic until soft.

In a deep stewing pot, bring chicken broth to a boil. Add all ingredients with the exception of the spinach. Boil gently for 45 minutes or until tender. Tear spinach in large pieces and add to stew a few minutes before serving. (Flour may be used to thicken the broth.)

Prince Edward Island (PEI)

Canada's smallest province is steeped in history and heritage. It is the "Birthplace of Confederation" because that is where the idea of Canada was born and where all federation documents were signed. It is the smallest province in both land area and population, with lush agricultural lands spread throughout. Historically, PEI is one of Canada's oldest settlements and demographically still reflects the oldest immigration to the country (Celtic, Anglo Saxon and French heritage). It is situated in the Gulf of St. Lawrence and separated from New Brunswick and Nova Scotia by the Northumberland Strait.

PEI's earliest settlers were the Mi'kmaqs known as Abegweit, meaning, "cradle in the waves." In 1534, Jacques Cartier deemed it "the fairest land that may possibly be seen."

PEI's deep brick red soil has always been its most striking feature. The population is predominantly British in origin, with a significant number of residents claiming French or Acadian heritage. The majority of the Acadian population can be traced to several hundred Acadians who escaped deportation at the time of the British occupation of the island following the fall of Louisburg in 1758.

People and supplies get to and from the island via the Confederation Bridge, which opened in May 1997. It links PEI to New Brunswick. At 12.9 km, it is the world's longest bridge over ice-covered water. The bridge is curved, designed to keep drivers alert and thus reduce accidents. The average crossing takes about ten minutes. It took four years to build and cost a total of $1 billion.

Our family has taken many ferry trips to PEI, however we did get to drive over the spectacular Confederation Bridge and loved the convenience of it (especially my grandchildren). Being a photographer, I love to scoop my hands in the soft red earth, capturing the rows of luscious verdant green potato leaves amongst the rusty red soil. The children especially love to smear their faces with the soil, which resembles bright war paint. Charlottetown, PEI's capital, is vibrant with colourful stores and artisan bistros. I especially liked the shop that sold delicious chocolate covered potato chips!

PEI is synonymous with potatoes, thus farming is the backbone of the economy. It produces approximately twenty-five per cent of Canada's quality potatoes.

PEI is also the home of "Anne of Green Gables", a fable made famous by Canadian author Lucy Maud Montgomery in 1908. She was made an Officer of the Order of the British Empire in 1935.

Canada's national treasure, singer/songwriter "Stompin" Tom Connors (who was named an Officer of the Order of Canada in 1996) gave a bit of notoriety to the small province. Although wide commercial appeal eluded him for much of his four-decade career, his songs like "The Hockey Song", "Canada Day", "Sudbury Saturday Night" and "Up Canada Way", have come to be regarded as national anthems.

But it was his song "Bud the Spud" that endeared him to PEI:

> *It's Bud the spud from the bright red mud*
> *Rollin' down the highway smiling.*
> *The spuds are big on the back of Bud's rig*
> *And they're from Prince Edward Island, they're from Prince Edward Island.*

It was 1972 when I first met Stomping Tom; he came rolling into the town of Bathurst for a gig. He parked his truck in the parking lot and threw down a piece of plywood. I asked him if he could move his truck as it was in the way. He said, "not before I'm done" and with that he took out his guitar and started singing "Bud the Spud" and stomped his right foot on the board to the beat of his own music. With splinters flying and the pure look of joy on his face, he was a fiercely proud Canadian, and that is what Canada is all about!

Ontario

In the early 1960s, our family was transferred to Trenton, Ontario, however we lived in nearby Brighton in Northumberland County, a small town that adhered to family values and simple country life. The church always played an important part in our lives so it was only natural that we became members of the Holy Angels Parish, a very small close-knit congregation. We shared our priest with Wooler, a neighbouring community. I presided over the Catholic Women's League. We cleaned the church, planted tulip bulbs in the spring, held bake sales and taught Catechism.

Northumberland County was the grandparent's home of a young Pauline Jewett, a Member of Parliament of the Canadian government. I can recall seeing her donning a pair of rubber gumboots and standing ankle deep in cow manure to shake hands with the local farmers. She campaigned long and hard urging people to vote Liberal under leader Lester B. Pearson.

As she entered each home she introduced herself as Dr. Pauline Jewett. One farmer seemed very pleased as he answered, "Come right on in ma'am, I've got a sick cow out back."

Despite her courageous efforts she lost the 1962 election, chalking it up as one of the worst disappointments she had ever endured. In February of 1963, a non-confidence vote in the government resulted in another general election. She ran once more as a Liberal in our Northumberland riding and won! She made women proud.

Northumberland County was a farming district, but I always referred to it as apple country, with its rolling hills and farms. On crisp fall days the maple leaves turned crimson, gold, amber and vermillion, and the slant of defused sunlight served notice that winter was not far behind.

On Saturdays, the children delighted in our country drives. With little noses pressed to the windows of the old Ford Fairlane we "Upsey Daisy... Downsey Daisey'd" over hill and dale as the dairy herds grazed lazily in the fields. One of my little daughters likened them to, "A handful of coloured raisins thrown on a green quilt."

Little apple stands freckled the winding roadside where farmers proudly presented the fruits of their labour. Large amber jugs of Applejack (cider), jars of creamy smooth apple butter, red candy apples and sparkling apple jellies stood on wooden barrels and crates. A bushel of McIntosh apples at that time could be had for one dollar. The farmer would upturn the basket into your car trunk, cascading apples over tire-jack, crowbar, and toys, blanketing the car with a heady fruitful aroma. The nippy Ontario fall freshened the apples so the taut skins would burst crisply at first bite, emitting sweet cool fresh juices that delighted the senses. This renowned apple was actually discovered in Ontario by John McIntosh who came upon the tree while clearing his land over 130 years ago!

With the car brimming with apple goodies and children savoring candy apples on a stick, the setting sun silhouetted a skein of wild Canada geese in a dramatic "V" formation against a raspberry sky, as we merrily "Upsey Daisy, Downsey Daisy'd" all the way home...

APPLE STREUSEL PIE

This is yummy decadent apple pie

STREUSEL

2/3 cup brown sugar
½ cup plus 2 tbsp flour
1 heaping tsp cinnamon

1 tsp nutmeg
⅛ tsp salt

FILLING

½ cup chilled butter
4½ cups Mac apples or other choice
½ cup sugar
4 tbsp flour
⅛ tsp salt
1 tsp cinnamon

1 large egg (beaten)
1 cup condensed milk
or heavy cream
1½ tsp Vanilla
1 unbaked single pie shell

In a large bowl, mix the first 6 ingredients by hand until crumbly. It should still have a slightly dry look to it. Set this streusel aside. Peel and core the apples, then slice thin to measure 4½ cups.

In a bowl mix the sugar flour and cinnamon. In a large bowl beat the egg then add the condensed milk or cream and vanilla. Add the sugar mixture and blend. Pour apples in this bowl of cream mixture and coat them well. Dump the entire apple mixture into the pie shell (without the streusel) and bake at 350°F for 25 minutes. *Then* sprinkle the streusel mixture over the pie.

Cook for another 40 minutes until puffy and golden brown.

This recipe calls for a 10-inch pie plate or flan pan.

ᰌ PANDORA ᰌ

**DRIVING TO CHURCH SERVICES—NANA K IS THE FIRST LADY IN
THE SECOND LAST ROW, BESIDE HER HUSBAND GEORGE**

While rummaging through my old cookbooks one day, I happened on a treasure of personal recipes of Nana K, my husband's grandmother. Tucked away in a thick folder, I found handwritten recipes that dated back to the turn of the century. Like many other cooks, she clipped newspaper and magazine articles for the perfect ladies club luncheon recipe and slipped them into an envelope, never to be seen again for decades.

Nana K, I was told, was an excellent cook, however I gathered this by just gleaning through her collection of recipes and the glowing reviews she had received. Nana K gained a bit of notoriety at the age of eighteen in 1903, when, with the help of her mother, entered a "Name the stove" contest, which was being promoted by the McClary Manufacturing Company. "This stove," the advertisement stated, "will be exquisite with many ingenious new devices for easing the work of cooking, reducing fuel bills, and preparing meals in a hurry. It had a compact and artistic appearance decidedly its own."

The contest was a very popular one, attracting some 20,000 contestants. Many names were submitted, but the most intriguing in the judge's estimation was the name "Pandora" submitted by none other than Nana K and two other contestants. In fairness, the McClary Manufacturing Company decided to award all three contestants with a brand new Pandora stove!

The black ornate stove remained in the family home on Cannon Street in Hamilton, Ontario for many years. Dr. Kerr, Nana K's eldest son, recalls the queue of stovepipes branching from Pandora's fiery core that were strung from the kitchen ceiling to facilitate heat, which prompted the following amusing story.

As a young boy he related how he bought a root beer kit from the store. He diligently followed the directions by adding yeast, sugar and root beer elixir. Nana K obliged and gave her young son the run of her kitchen. He pushed and tightened the corks into the bottles, then tied each one securely with butcher string. They were then stored in the basement for fermenting.

The required maturing time had lapsed and now it was time for the long-awaited moment. Retrieving a bottle, which he had sitting next to Pandora, he calmly sat at the kitchen table and examined its contents. Carefully he untied the string, when without warning, a tremendous force shot the cork out like a canon straight upward and clear through the thinning stovepipe, spewing a shower of black cinders all over the kitchen table! Pandora's revenge. Nana K was not amused to say the very least!

The same young lad, (who turned out to be my father-in-law) after being educated at the University of Toronto, went on to open the Department of Medicine at the University of British Columbia in 1950. He also was the recipient of the Order of the British Empire.

My mother-in-law, Lois Kerr was a renaissance woman with many fortes, however, cooking was not one of them. In her kitchen a plaque hung for all to see, "The kitchen is closed due to illness – I'm sick of cooking." Vacating the kitchen gave Lois ample time to follow her dreams. As a young journalist for the *Globe & Mail* in Toronto, she interviewed Amelia Earhart before her attempted but fatal transatlantic flight around the world. She was an author, playwright, songwriter, and mother of three successful sons. John is a professional Geological Engineer, who completed a career in the mineral exploration business. James is a meteorologist who shared acknowledgement for his contribution of scientific data with Vice President Al Gore's Nobel Peace Prize on Climate Change. Charles is a medical doctor specializing in Cardiology at St Paul's Hospital in Vancouver.

The only cooking prowess that Lois had, was cooking roast beef every Sunday, accompanied by baked potatoes and frozen peas!

NANA K'S (SECRET) ORANGE SPONGE CAKE RECIPE

With cream cheese frosting

This famous Kerr recipe brings back fond memories for my husband, John when as a young boy home on vacation from Upper Canada College, he worked with the Canadian Pacific Railway as a "Newsie." He rented pillows, sold cigarettes, pop, and snacks. It was a lucrative job for a fifteen-year-old but he felt it would be even more so if he could convince his Nana K, who was vacationing in Vancouver from Hamilton, Ontario at the time, to make him some of her delicious sponge cake to sell. For a month, the passengers of the CPR from Vancouver to Calgary relished Nana K's Orange Sponge Cake and so did young John — all the way to the bank!

This orange cake recipe was a closely guarded secret and never indulged to any family member. It is over 120 years old! I, however, will not reveal how I garnered her recipe. Enjoy!

6 egg yolks
1½ cups orange juice
Finely grated orange rind from 2
oranges
3 cups sugar

3 cups flour
2 tsp baking powder
1 tsp salt
6 egg whites

In a large bowl, beat the egg yolks with the orange juice and rind until foamy. Slowly add the sugar, while beating.

Sift the dry ingredients together. Fold the flour into the egg yolk mixture with a rubber spatula with a cut and fold-over motion.

Beat the egg whites until stiff but not dry. Carefully *fold* (this is important) the egg whites into the batter until well blended (same cut and fold-over method).

Pour into a large floured, *ungreased* tube cake pan (the cake will not adhere to the sides if greased). Some tube pans are smaller than others. Fill 2/3 full (if you have batter remaining just fill a pie plate or small baking pan and insert in the oven along with the cake) Bake between 300-325°F for 65 minutes or when the middle of the cake looks done (the smaller cake will be cooked much sooner). Invert the pan (it won't fall out!) and cool for one hour before loosening the sides of the cake and slide onto a plate. This recipe may be halved.

Failures of sponge cakes are due to too slow an oven and greasing the pan or taking them out of the oven before they are thoroughly baked.

CREAM CHEESE ICING

4 oz cream cheese
4 oz unsalted butter
1½ tsp vanilla

2 cups icing sugar (or more depending on desired thickness)
Finely grated orange
rind from 1 orange

This recipe may be doubled.

In a large bowl beat cheese and butter until creamy with electric mixer. While beating on low speed, add the icing sugar and beat until fluffy. Add the grated orange rind and vanilla and beat until blended. Frost cake.

Manitoba

Portage la Prairie is situated on the Assiniboine River west of Winnipeg. My five years on the prairies were engaging ones. My first impression of the prairies was how large the sky was! One could drive all day and never see a mountain or hill. From a distance, a grain elevator would suddenly appear and in the blink of an eye, you could see the empty boxcars beside them, telling whether the crop was wheat, flax, rye, barley, or whether the farmer was threshing, seeding, baling or stooking hay.

Manitoba encompasses a great variety of geographical settings, social structures and climatic conditions. Ask anyone who has stood in Winnipeg on the corner of Portage and Main in January how cold it is! Beside its harsh winters and flat land, there is no spectacle more breathtaking than that of the prairie sun setting on a rhythmic sea of waving wheat, or the sweet smell of freshly mown hay.

The western communal families of the Mennonites and Hutterites are very intriguing. The Hutterites are the largest family-type communal living group in the western world. They are noted for successful large-scale farming and effective training of the young. The women work and plough side by side with their husbands. Their reward is the knowledge that they are serving their Lord in the most perfect manner. Perhaps the thought of a bolt of calico to sew up a new raft of dresses; aprons and polka dotted babushkas urged them forward too. So as not to cause discord among the womenfolk, women and children wear coinciding cotton frocks.

There was a well-scrubbed, healthy glow about them as cherub cheeked toddlers hung on to the long flowing skirts of their young mothers... clinging to a heritage that has retained solidarity despite the persecutions of surrounding neighbours.

Portage la Prairie was our first posting. Our family settled on the air force base in a PMQ (Private Married Quarters).

In keeping with fulfilling my Christian duties as outlined in the Ecumenical Council, I presided over most positions in the Catholic Women's League and the Christian Family Movement. With all these committees, I left a trail of notch gavels, and "Dainty" recipes for bake sales, cookbooks and bazaars. In these, I always included my own family recipes, from Acadian, Québec, and Maritime culture. The favourite recipe question asked of me was, "What in the world is a Blueberry Grunt?"

Winnipeg is known for its diverse ethnic cuisine. What would the prairies be without recipes like: Goldeye, a rose coloured fleshed fish that is found in Manitoba's northern lake; Creamy Mennonite Onion Pie or German cabbage rolls topped with ginger snaps?

HUTTERITE CABBAGE ROLLS

The spice and gingersnaps make this recipe unique! Time: 1½ hours

FILLING

1 lb lean ground beef	1 egg beaten
1 large onion (chopped)	3 cloves garlic (minced)
1 tbsp butter	½ tsp salt
1 cup cooked rice	

SAUCE

2- 14 oz cans tomato sauce	⅛ tsp ground clove
1 cup water (I add a chicken	¼ tsp allspice
bouillon cube for more flavor)	Salt and pepper to taste
1 small onion (chopped)	1 small can of sauerkraut
2 tbsp brown sugar	6–8 gingersnaps crushed
1 bay leaf	1 large cabbage

Sauce: (Some canned tomato sauces are salted; therefore check before adding more salt). Combine sauce ingredients with the exception of the gingersnaps. Mix well in a medium sized saucepan and simmer (uncovered) for about 30 minutes.

In a large kettle, cover cabbage with water and simmer for 15 minutes. Remove cabbage, drain and cool slightly. Remove leaves, spread on a cloth and cool completely and set aside.

Filling: Sauté the onion and butter until soft. (This is to remove the boiled onion taste.) In a bowl combine the sautéed onions, uncooked ground beef and the rest of the ingredients.

Stuff 8 leaves with the meat mixture. Roll tightly starting from the thin end, tucking ends neatly starting from the thin end. Some use toothpicks for this however if you lay it properly it shouldn't be difficult.

Cover bottom of casserole with a little of the sauce and cabbage leaves. Top with the stuffed rolls and cover with remaining sauce. Pour sauerkraut over sauce. Cover with tin foil and bake for 30 minutes.

Uncover and add crushed gingersnaps. Bake uncovered for an additional 35 minutes or until golden brown.

Serves 6–8 people.

MENNONITE ONION PIE

Preheat oven to 400°F

3 tbsp butter

2 cups sliced onions

1 clove crushed garlic

1 uncooked pie shell

½ cup Swiss cheese

4 eggs

2 cups of half and half cream

¼ tsp dry mustard

¼ tsp nutmeg

½ tsp salt

1 dash Tabasco sauce

Sauté the onions and garlic in butter until limp and transparent. Arrange them in an uncooked pie shell. Cover with grated cheese. Beat eggs. Add remaining ingredients and stir well. Pour beaten eggs over onions. Bake on lowest rack of the oven for 15 minutes. Lower temperature to 325°F and bake an additional 30 minutes or when the middle seems firm, and the top is a golden brown.

The nostalgic memories of Winnipeg in the 1950s for me meant looking for:

- The Long Tramp Mural that said "54 miles to Portage la Prairie". A sign that probably dates back to the mid-1930s

- Mayor Stephen Juba (1957-1977)

- The Royal Winnipeg Ballet (founded in 1939)

- *All you can eat for $1.99* (Buffet on Main Street in Winnipeg – 1957)

- Winnipeg's famous "Golden Boy" statue. He was gilded in 24-carat gold then lifted to his perch in 1919 facing north on the Manitoba Legislative Building

- *"Moss I Gather"* (Winnipeg Free Press column to which I submitted and published poetry, and limping limericks)

- Bud Grant (Coach of the Winnipeg Blue Bombers 1957-1966)

- St. Boniface Cathedral (Mother Church of Western Canada, est. 1818)

On weekends it was "off to Grandma's house we'd go." Grandma and Grandpa in this case were my first husband's grandparents. They lived in Marquette, a farming community about twenty-five miles west of Winnipeg.

My favourite memories are the sight of Grandma Fleury (her name was Louise). She was born in Jamestown, Michigan, a plump fair-skinned gentle woman with dark brown eyes, as she huddled over the bake board kneading bread. She made no sound but could jolt you with her smile. On the other hand Grandpa David Winter Fleury was a hard working labouring man of French descent. He reminded me of a huge tree with an appetite to match.

Grandma's kitchen had wooden cupboards and sideboards, and a black and silver wood-stove that was fired all year round. When the top cooled slightly, wax paper was rubbed on its surface, thus melting the paraffin and buffing it to an ebony-like shine. At the north end stood the gleaming white sink and stand that Grandpa retrieved (or so he said) for "Weezie" (his pet name for Grandma). "It just floated on by so I brought it home," he said with a mischievous grin. He was referring to the Red River flood in 1950.

The long kitchen table was large enough to accommodate the hired hands during threshing season. It had a faded rose-patterned oilcloth that was scored with fine cuts where the bread knife missed its mark. The centre was the focal point for condiments of sugar, molasses, mustard, salt, pepper, butter and a glass of teaspoons, all protected with a clean soft muslin cloth.

Under the table was a square door, with an attached iron ring. Pulling upwards on the ring opened the door to the cool root cellar, with its cobwebs and earthy musk smells. A pull on the suspended light bulb with dangling chain exposed shiny Mason jars of mustard pickles, chows and relishes. Jams and jellies of wild huckleberry, blueberry, raspberry, strawberry and her famous Saskatoon berry preserve, stood in paraffin topped glasses like bright jewels. Their contents were ready to be plucked and surrendered to a thick slice of homemade bread.

The Saskatoon berry, which grows wild in the fields, is native to the prairies. It's reminiscent of an overgrown blueberry. When full, they get plump and juicy, an excellent combination for luscious prairie pie! Grandma Fleury was definitely a nest builder and the heart of that nest was under her kitchen table!

The farm's backyard was overrun with daisies and buttercups. They spilled onto the back stoop near a unique boot scraper made out of upturned bottle caps nailed to a board. Next to the stoop, is where I washed my baby's flannelette diapers. They were washed the "environmentally friendly" way, on a metal scrub board in the soft rainwater that I collected from the wooden barrel by the drainpipe. I would peg them all on a line outside and prop a long pole in the middle, pushing them skyward to catch the warm summer breezes. Standing back I proudly marveled as they dazzled and danced and watched the clothes fairies as they busily flapped the corners into frazzled knots. What I didn't peg out, I lay out in the tall grass and watched the brilliant sun kiss tiny cotton dresses, lace bonnets, socks and blankets. I shared this splendour with the occasional chicken who curiously pecked at the brightly coloured buttons.

With hand on hip and babe on the other, I drew in the fresh unspoiled country air. I looked down and smiled at my youngest daughter and said, "Yep, some day you will have a washer and dryer little sweetie, and you will have missed all of this," and with the intuition of her gender, she just smiled a wide toothy grin.

Grandma Fleury also showed me how to churn butter the old fashioned way in an old empty gallon size "Rogers white syrup" can. She filled it with pure cream from the separator, and then told me to rock it gently back and forth. After an hour of splish-splash, it seemed to have seized on me as nothing was happening. This must have been the best part I guessed from Grandma Fleury's grin. All at once to my surprise, I heard a very wet "splosh" and "kaplunk" as the cream had separated from the whey and the butter was slamming against the end of the can. We opened the can and retrieved the golden fat. We washed it under the pipe as I pumped fresh well water over it and removed all traces of whey. We then used the reserved buttermilk for a batch of pancakes the next morning.

The early sounds of roosters announcing the break of dawn, and the burning aroma of wood, gently nudged the senses. Uncle Johnny stoked the fires. The thud of another armful of wood hitting the floor was a welcome sound as the little ones giggled as they peeked shyly around the stairs. This meant perhaps he would entertain them with his funny faces and toothy gapped grin. I could blissfully sleep for an extra fifteen minutes, lost in the warm cozy layers of Grandma's quilts.

Grandma patiently taught me how to make her marvelous golden hot biscuits. Her unique biscuit cutter was an old baking powder can that had its top and bottom removed. It was so worn that the edges were razor sharp and it cut biscuits with little effort. It also doubled as a doughnut cutter, while a thimble inserted in the middle of the dough made a perfect hole. This is her recipe.

BAKING POWDER BISCUITS

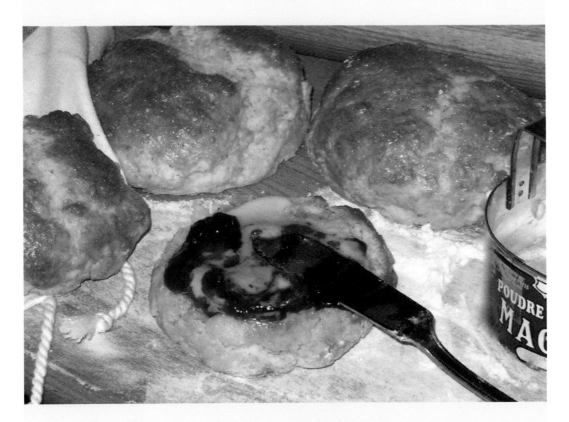

2 cups unbleached flour
4 tsp baking powder
1 tsp salt
1½ tsp sugar

⅓ cup shortening or butter
1 cup milk
1 egg (for glazing)

Set oven at 450°F. Combine flour, baking powder and salt, sugar and blend. With pastry cutter (or hands, as Grandma preferred) mix until it resembles coarse cornmeal.

Make a dent in the middle and add the milk all at once. Working quickly, scrape the sides of the bowl until you have a solid mass.

Put dough on a floured board and mix and pat slightly (the secret is not to work the dough too much). Roll dough lightly to 1½ to 2-inch thickness.

Cut dough with a floured cutter (I use a floured drinking glass). Place on a greased cookie sheet and brush the tops with beaten whole egg. Bake in hot oven at 450°F for 15 minutes, or until golden brown.

British Columbia

∽ FRASER GOLD HORSEFLY ∾

After many years of living in Canada's picturesque Eastern Provinces, and with my family grown, my former husband and I went our separate ways. I then moved to British Columbia where, I remarried and now enjoy the mining life with my husband John, a Geological Engineer. Vancouver, is where we call home, a breathtakingly beautiful city with balmy temperatures and lots of rain, is a place where you just don't tan... you rust!

A drilling program was due to start in the spring. The regular camp cook couldn't make it. Being shorthanded, John asked me if I would like to do some cooking; I jumped at the chance!

Williams Lake (Willy's puddle, as my husband affectionately calls it) is about 340 miles (548 km) northeast of Vancouver, British Columbia. It's the home of Rick Hansen, of "Man in Motion" fame, and BC's largest rodeo – the Williams Lake Stampede – which attracts people from all over western Canada and the United States.

About half an hour (as the crow flies), east of Williams Lake is the curious little town of Horsefly (yes that's its actual name). This settlement was originally called Harper's Camp after Thaddeus Harper, pioneer rancher and miner, where the proliferous summer flies not only bite they "whinny."

As original as its name implies, so are the diversified townsfolk. The sparsely populated town has a sort of magnetic charm to it luring artists, poets and writers from hither and yon.

It is with great amusement that I recall one afternoon sitting in the local restaurant when a dispute ensued. A gentleman diner informed the proprietress that due to a financial embarrassment he was unable to pay for his delicious meal. He would therefore compensate her with a "literary" gift. He then stood smartly, and recited thirteen verses from "The Man from Snowy River!" He left the establishment with rousing applause from the dining guests ringing merrily in his ears!

At the end of the logger's road that winds its way up the beautiful Horsefly River, past Jacobson's Camp, is the majestic MacKay River Valley. As you follow the breathtaking mountain range, you come upon a mining property called Fraser Gold owned jointly by my husband John's company, Eureka Resources Inc. We 'roughed it' there, with all the tenacity of the Beverly Hillbillies. The kitchen trailer was painted sparkling white with an abundance of shelves. The kitchen had all the amenities of home. A six-burner stove and grill, a large stainless steel steamer, two sinks, a large freezer and two fridges.

The cutout doors let the fresh mountain air in and it opened to a large verandah, made of 2x4s. There, my herb garden of basil, savory, chives, and dill grew wild in their surroundings. Marigolds, petunias, and primroses cascaded from their pots, spilling onto the railing.

From the pencil-topped spruce trees, the beautiful snow-capped Eureka Peak shimmered like sugar-dusted meringue in the noonday sun!

Baking bread was hilarious at first, as I hadn't adjusted the amount of yeast to compensate for the 4,200 foot altitude. Every time I looked back at the overflowing pan, the dough kept threateningly creeping towards me as if posing to attack! Decreasing the amount of yeast remedied the problem, but not before getting a good teasing from the crew.

My assistant cook had cabin fever and left without notice, so I had to hire someone quick. After many interviews, I finally set my sights on this lovely lady with much experience. She had been camp cook for, as she put it, "about one hundred years." She settled in, and I was delighted. The crew wanted to know all about her. She then told us she was Rick Hansen's biological mother, the world famous Man in Motion. We were delighted.

We set out plans for making wheelchair ramps in case of a surprise visit. Alas, things didn't turn out that way as she was not feeling well and had to leave. At a function a year later, I met Rick Hansen in Vancouver and told him of our encounter with his mother. He smiled and said, "Yep, and she's a darn good camp cook!"

THE CHRISTMAS GIFT

"A catered gourmet dinner prepared by myself for four people, that's the perfect gift," I said to my husband. We had planned everyone's Christmas gift with the exception of his brother Dr. Charles Kerr and his wife Karen. Being head of Cardiology at the University

Hospital in Vancouver, Charles was as much attached to his pager as Karen was to their children. I thought this gift would come as a welcomed relief for both of them.

On Christmas day, they opened their gift. A gilt-edged card announced the forthcoming present: "A catered gourmet dinner for an evening and couple of their choice, to be redeemed at any time." The menu:

Coquilles St-Jacques
Plump local scallops in a creamy wine sauce
crowned with velvet-fluted potatoes

Salt Springs Quail
Stuffed with fruited wild rice and brandied sauce

Potatoes Dauphine
Asparagus with Béarnaise sauce

Home-baked French baguette

Chestnut Crème Coronet
Choux pastry filled with chestnut cream
drizzled with Belgian chocolate

They were ecstatic! "What a unique idea!" Karen kept saying. Three weeks later, a call from Karen redeeming her Christmas gift lifted my spirits as I wondered who her guests would be and do they like quail!

"Not to worry, I have the perfect couple, and I'm sure they like French food."

"Who?" I asked impatiently.

"Vancouver's mayor, His Worship — although we didn't call him that — Gordon Campbell, and his wife Nancy."

I was comfortable with the fact that the Campbell's were to be their guests since Charles and Gordon were childhood friends, and best man to each other's weddings.

We arrived about six-thirty. The guests had arrived, and were sitting comfortably around the fireplace having cocktails. "Kerr's Catering!" I called out jokingly, and marched briskly to the kitchen with skillet in hand. Nancy smiled quizzically, and Gordon was up on his feet following me into the kitchen (Karen had not informed them that I was coming). "It's a pleasant surprise," she said explaining the gift. Meanwhile Gordon was sticking his fingers in the pots.

"Out of my kitchen!" I ordered laughingly. He smiled and asked, "What are you cooking?"

"Roast quail and brandied sauce," I answered.

"I hate quail," he said.

"You what?"

"Just kidding!" he grinned.

We chatted a while and they asked us to join them, as we hadn't seen the Campbells in a while. We had dinner reservations elsewhere, saying "perhaps another time."

I served the Coquilles St-Jacques, piping hot as a starter. I made a mock one out of veal for Charlie, as he does not like seafood – much to the delight of my husband who dined on the extra coquille!

The main course was the quail, Brandied sauce, and wild rice, Potatoes Dauphine, asparagus tips with Béarnaise sauce, and hot crusty French bread.

During all this, the family's two black cats eyed me with reservation as if questioning my presence.

I took out the Crème Chestnut ring dessert, and lay it on the cupboard. In two seconds Rock Crusher – one of the family cats – pounced up for a closer sniff. "Gotcha!" I put him down and looked at my watch. *It's time for our own reservations,* I thought. John was reluctant to leave the table as he diligently mopped a last tiny morsel of scallop with a hot piece of bread.

Nancy was very impressed with the dinner and thanked us both. Gordon walked us to the door and said it was the best dinner he's had out in a long time and was looking forward to dessert.

"What a wonderful evening," I said to my husband, as we sat sipping a cocktail and relaxing in a fine Vancouver restaurant. It reminded me of the days of *La Corbeille,* (my French restaurant) when we catered for private parties. *The dinner was a complete success,* I thought as I took another sip of wine – then almost choked!

"What's the matter?" John asked.

"Rock Crusher!" I yelled and ran to the pay phone. I had visions of Crusher's head and flea collar deep into the creamy Chestnut dessert with his black tail swaying in ecstasy!

"Hello... Karen?"

"No, Jeannette. It didn't happen. He restrained himself," she said with a laugh.

"You must have read my mind," I breathed with relief.

"Besides, I put it in the cupboard to finish thawing, we're eating it now and it's absolutely marvelous. Nancy and Gordon thank you again," she added, "It was the most unique gift ever!"

When I returned to the table and told John what had not happened, he raised his glass and made a toast, "To Rock Crusher who knew better."

Gordon Campbell went on to be the Premier of British Columbia. He has since been appointed as the High Commissioner to the United Kingdom and Northern Ireland and at present, resides in London, England.

COQUILLES ST-JACQUES À LA CORBEILLE

1½ lbs large sea or Bay scallops
1 cup white table wine or chicken broth
2 tsp tarragon
½ tsp salt
3 tbsp butter
2 cups chopped (fine) mushrooms

2 large cloves of garlic (minced)
3 tbsp shallots
3 tbsp butter
3 tbsp flour
½ cup light cream
¾ cup grated Gruyère or Swiss cheese

Lightly grease six coquille shells or ceramic shells with butter. Place on a 15x10x1 inch pan.

Carefully rinse scallops in cold water. In a medium-sized saucepan, place scallops, wine, tarragon and salt. Add just enough water to cover scallops.

Heat to boiling, reduce to simmer for about 4 minutes or until scallops are *almost* done (do not overcook)

Remove scallops with a slotted spoon and put aside. Boil remaining liquid and reduce to measure 1 cup. Strain liquid and reserve.

In same pan, sauté mushrooms and green onions or shallots for about 6 minutes stirring occasionally until tender. Remove from pan.

In same saucepan melt the next 3 tablespoons of butter. Stir in the flour, cook briskly until smooth. Gradually stir in reserved liquid. Heat to boiling stirring briskly. Cook for 1 minute. Stir in the cream and mushroom mixture. Correct the seasoning. If mixture gets too thick, add more cream.

Divide the scallops evenly among 6 large coquille shells or ceramic shells. Evenly pour the mushroom mixture over the scallops.

Pipe mashed potatoes that have a creamy consistency into rosettes around the coquilles. Grate the cheese in the centre of the coquilles. Place under broiler until the potato rosette tips are golden and the cheese has bubbled and golden.

Canada's North

∽ THE LAND OF THE MIDNIGHT SUN ∽

Although my experience with Canada's north is rather limited, I had three wonderful experiences in the land of the midnight sun. One is in the city of Whitehorse, latitude 60 degrees N, the capital and largest city of the Yukon Territory. The Guinness World Book of Records deemed Whitehorse as the city with the least air pollution in the world. The name "Whitehorse" is derived from the common term for whitecap or cresting wave that resembled a white horse with flowing mane.

In the late 1980s, I visited my daughter who lived in Whitehorse. She and her family led a very pristine life in the Yukon. They hunted and fished and had a yard full of Huskies, which they hitched to their dog sled in the winter and "mushed" everywhere. Moose and elk are the mainstay of most diets, and in the fall, freezers are filled with moose meat and berries.

I recall my visit to the Yukon, when with excitement I met my youngest at the Whitehorse airport. With long hair that fell in a youthful flair, plaid shirt, jeans, Mukluks, and an exuberant longing for the great outdoors, she integrated into Yukon life very well I thought. We laughed and hugged, she wondered what was in the box that I so carefully guarded on the plane. It was of course some lobster from Shediac, New Brunswick. She was ecstatic and could hardly wait to reach home to feast on it. I took such pleasure in cooking for her while she worked at the local vet's facility in the city. In her log cabin home, I kneaded batches of homemade bread, moose balls, meat pies, cookies and pastries and filled her freezer for the winter.

My inner clock must have been off kilter as I woke up to a beautiful afternoon, or so I thought. The family wondered what all the clanging of pots and pans in the kitchen at three o'clock in the morning was – not that it endeared me to my dear daughter, who had to be at work in just a few hours! It then occurred to me that the sun never sets during the summer equinox.

I was reminded of my other experience in the far north; my husband and I were on a mining venture on the east coast of Greenland, near the small community of Mestersvig, latitude 72 degrees N. Although not Canada, Greenland has the very same environment.

In our Weatherhaven tent one night, there was a stillness in the air as the sun cast bright glints off the glacial ice, it was so breathtaking that I decided to hike out and look for Musk Ox wool. I was in awe of the pristine tundra that was carpeted with wildflowers. I found many clumps of wool, which had been rubbed off onto the rocks by the large Musk Ox. It wasn't long before an ATV came roaring towards me, as I had strayed over a mile from camp. "Do you know it's three in the morning and also, there have been polar bear and Musk Ox sightings near camp?" the geologist informed me. It didn't take much coaxing to jump onto the revving vehicle while clutching my prized possession, a large bag of Musk Ox wool and my second exciting venture in the land of the midnight sun!

Other than Whitehorse, this north was just as exhilarating.

Pinned to the Christmas tree this exciting morn was a curious envelope with my name written on a red coloured envelope. I, of course ripped it open and found this wonderful gift from my benevolent husband John, which was a fabulous trip to Churchill, Manitoba to photograph wild polar bears from a Tundra buggy (Frontier North Adventures) in November 2011. I was ecstatic, a photographer's dream! Canada's Churchill, Manitoba, which is about eighty miles from the Nunavut/ Manitoba boundary, is known as the "Polar bear capital of the world."

On arrival in Churchill, I first climbed aboard a helicopter and captured the bears sleeping in sea kelp and huddled underneath trees. The bears were waiting for Hudson Bay to freeze over. Winter was late this year. I had visions of mountains of snow and ice however the snow was sparse but the weather was very cold. The tundra buggy is a well-equipped vehicle; its tires are 5½ feet high and 3½ feet wide. The average polar bear is between six to ten feet in height.

The main lodge is a five-module buggy, which contains the sleeping quarters, dining room and lounge. The sleeping accommodations are bunk bed style and rather intimate. Every bed has a window and one could peek out and see polar bears sniffing about, which made one feel quite snug and safe tucked in your top bunk with warm blankets. The guide however, was telling us that it wasn't up to snuff to the likes of Martha Stewart who brought her own designer sheets and pillows!

"HAPPINESS IS..."

In the early morning, after a wholesome hot breakfast we loaded onto the single-unit tundra buggy for the day. We were all so excited, and we were not disappointed. After about a half hour of travelling we came upon an Arctic fox that looked magnificent against some dark rocks. Not too far beyond, we happened on a couple of large polar bears lumbering along sniffing the air. What a thrill!

They looked so huge and so cuddly but if by some misfortune you happen to fall out of that buggy at their feet, you can be certain that you would be nothing but a snack of Canadian bacon to them!

Excitement mounted, cameras clicked, and people jostled for the best window position. I sprinted forward (like any obnoxious photographer) but was suddenly held back by this lady I had met earlier – Mariko, a lovely deaf/mute woman from Japan who was in a panic. Her camera was stuck! Tears streaming down her face she motioned for help. "Quickly," she gestured, "before they go away."

My first instincts were to just buffalo ahead. I looked sheepishly away. No one helped, but those flailing arms with all that camera gear got to me. I reluctantly caved. I helped her with her camera and wondered *why does this always happen to me?* I could hear everyone "oohing" and "awwwing" at the bears up front. Mariko went to her allotted seat for the impaired near the driver.

I felt so cheated. Then I turned around to the back of the buggy and what I saw was astounding. There were two bears nestled lovingly in the gently falling snow, no one saw them but me! Alone, I slowly lifted my camera and leisurely shot at my beautiful subjects. It was the only photograph taken of that scene on that day. (I know, I checked!) After the bears had left someone called my name, I turned around to see Mariko snapping my picture after which she bowed profusely and thanked me many times over. Mariko was a very talented and artistic photographer and she did get some prolific shots. We kept in touch. Moral of the story "don't let a good deed go unchecked for it may end up to being one of nature's best gifts!"

The polar Bears of Churchill

JEANNETTE, COMPLIMENTS OF PHOTOGRAPHER MARIKO

Epilogue

Through these pages my life unfolded with childlike, tongue-in-cheek abandon. Many of the characters are no longer living, but I keep them in the corridors of my mind and open the doors occasionally, and nostalgically hear Silver Jack crooning "Danny Boy". Roseanne singing *"le bonhomme et la bonne femme"*. My brother Johnny, "He shoots….he sco-o-ores!" Beaverbrook's "Enjoy the simplicity of it". Mr. Rosenberg's "Shalom", Mo's mischievous words, "Don't forget to cross your fingers". The singsong of little voices …"Upsey daisy, downsey daisy… all the way home".

Time is most elusive. In retrospect, of all the years that have fled by, I've seen the tides of change. In my time, the Berlin Wall crumbled, as well as Communism in the eastern European bloc and USSR. There have been no world wars since, but here in Canada, the internal strife we have witnessed developing between our Québec neighbours is quite disconcerting. It is not too farfetched to compare it to a simmering volcano waiting to erupt at any given moment.

Not since July 24, 1967 when Canada heard General Charles de Gaulle's rebel call from the balcony of Montréal's City Hall of, "*Vive Ie Québec Libre*," has Québec and the rest of Canada's relations been quite the same. The phrase has often been coined by Québec's French sovereigntists to further their cause. The Canadian referendum on Canadian Unity/ Senate reform, and acknowledgement of Québec as a distinct society, implemented by the Progressive Conservative government, was defeated May 20th,1980.

At time of writing, Justin Pierre James Trudeau, son of Pierre Elliot Trudeau has his eye on the prize. On April 14, 2013, Justin Trudeau was elected leader of the Liberal Party. Stephen Harper is the 22nd and current Prime Minister of Canada and leader of the Conservative Party. Thomas Mulcair is leader of the federal NDP Party, which is the official opposition, representing the socialist society of Canadian politics.

Canada is a federal parliamentary democracy and a constitutional monarchy, Queen Elizabeth II being the current head of state. Canada is a member of the British Commonwealth of Nations; is officially bilingual federally; is a very diverse multi-cultured country; and is one of the wealthiest countries in the world.

In total area it is the world's second largest country. Its common border with the United States of America forms the world's longest land border. Canada is a North American country consisting of ten provinces and three territories. From these provinces and territories was the nucleus for this book.

Someday perhaps we can all unite collectively and feast on the recipes that brought this great country called Canada together. Like the recipes found in this book, they are all authentic and all have been in great families for generations. Use them in good health and remember:

When all is written down
And said,
One thing's for certain,
There's still sliced bread!

MONTREAL STAIRCASES BY KRYS HARTLE

POUR MOI.
THESE THINGS I LOVE.

An elegant table - with
Snow-white cloth
Candescent reflections
that scintillate off
old -world crystal and
Porcelain plates,
French table service
for dinner at eight…
Pour moi these things I love.

Pâté de fois gras in
Cumberland sauce
café-au-lait served
demi-tasse.
Friends round the table,
decorum refined,
baguette of French bread
and Beaujolais wine.
Pour moi, these things I love.

But a bustling Kitchen
cloyed with din,
where barefoot
toddlers play within
its jam-flecked floor
and crayoned walls.
Pour moi my heart
loves most of all!

—Jeannette Kerr

PHOTOS & CREDITS

Lord Beaverbrook Image:
by I R Walker 2008

Observation Car:
CT Trolley Museum
A special thanks to web editor, J (Joe) E Smith
Photographed by Frank Rossino

Montreal streets:
Watercolour by Krys Hartle

Composite of Little Girl in Red River Coat:
by Jeannette Kerr

Recipes in Maple syrup section:
The Bernier Family (Mrs. Claire Ormiston)

Recipes:
Prepared and Photographed by Jeannette Kerr

CPSIA information can be obtained
at www.ICGtesting.com
Printed in the USA
LVIC04n2255230915

455461LV00006B/6